ISBN 978-3-409-12447-8   ISBN 978-3-322-90995-4
DOI 10.1007/ 978-3-322-90995-4

Journal of International  Business

Special Issue
2/2003

Management International Review

Niels G. Noorderhaven (Guest Editor)
Can Multinationals Bridge the Gap Between Global and Local?
Guest Editor's Introduction

Manuel Becerra/Juan Santaló
An Empirical Analysis of the Corporate Effect in MNCs

Alfredo J. Mauri/Rakesh B. Sambharya
Performance Implications of Global Integration

Niels G. Noorderhaven/Anne-Wil Harzing
Country-of-origin Effect in MNCs

Peter J. Buckley/Jeremy Clegg/Hui Tan
Knowledge Transfer in China

Fiona Moore
Branch/Head Office Relations in a Financial MNC

D 21247

EDITORIAL BOARD

Professor Raj Aggarwal, Kent State University, Kent – U.S.A.
Professor Jeffrey S. Arpan, University of South Carolina, Columbia – U.S.A.
Professor Daniel van Den Bulcke, Universiteit Antwerpen – Belgium
Professor John A. Cantwell, University of Reading – United Kingdom
Professor S. Tamer Cavusgil, Michigan State University, East Lansing – U.S.A.
Professor Frederick D.S. Choi, New York University – U.S.A.
Professor Farok Contractor, Rutgers University, Newark – U.S.A.
Professor John D. Daniels, University of Miami, Coral Gables – U.S.A.
Professor Peter J. Dowling, University of Canberra – Australia
Professor Santiago García Echevarría, Universidad de Alcála de Henares, Madrid – Spain
Professor Lawrence A. Gordon, University of Maryland, College Park – U.S.A.
Professor Sidney J. Gray, University of New South Wales, Sydney – Australia
Professor Geir Gripsrud, Norwegian School of Management, Sandvika – Norway
Professor Jean-François Hennart, Tilburg University – The Netherlands
Professor Georges Hirsch, Centre Franco-Vietnamien de Formation à la gestion, Paris – France
Professor Neil Hood, University of Strathclyde, Glasgow – United Kingdom
Professor Andrew Inkpen, Thunderbird, The American Graduate School of International Management, Glendale – U.S.A.
Professor Eugene D. Jaffe, Bar-Ilan University, Ramat-Gan – Israel
Professor Erdener Kaynak, Pennsylvania State University, Middletown – U.S.A.
Professor Yui Kimura, University of Tsukuba, Tokyo – Japan
Professor Michael Kutschker, Katholische Universität Eichstätt, Ingolstadt – Germany
Professor Reijo Luostarinen, Helsinki School of Economics – Finland
Professor Klaus Macharzina, Universität Hohenheim, Stuttgart – Germany
Professor Roger Mansfield, Cardiff Business School – United Kingdom
Professor Mark Mendenhall, University of Tennessee, Chattanooga – U.S.A.
Professor Rolf Mirus, University of Alberta, Edmonton – Canada
Professor Michael H. Moffett, American Graduate School, Phoenix – U.S.A.
Professor Krzysztof Y. Obloj, University of Warsaw – Poland
Professor Lars Oxelheim, Lund University – Sweden
Professor Ki-An Park, Kyung Hee University, Seoul – Korea
Professor Robert D. Pearce, University of Reading – United Kingdom
Professor Lee Radebaugh, Brigham Young University, Provo – U.S.A.
Professor Wolf Reitsperger, Universität Hamburg – Germany
Professor Edwin Rühli, Universität Zürich – Switzerland
Professor Alan M. Rugman, Indiana University, Bloomington, U.S.A.
Professor Rakesh B. Sambharya, Rutgers University, Camden, U.S.A.
Professor Reinhart Schmidt, Universität Halle-Wittenberg – Germany
Professor Hans Schöllhammer, University of California, Los Angeles – U.S.A.
Professor Oded Shenkar, The Ohio State University, Columbus – U.S.A.
Professor Vitor Corado Simoes, Universidade Técnica de Lisboa – Portugal
Professor John Stopford, 6 Chalcot Square, London NW1 8YB – United Kingdom
Professor Daniel P. Sullivan, University of Delaware, Newark – U.S.A.
Professor Norihiko Suzuki, International Christian University, Tokyo – Japan
Professor Stephen Bruce Tallmann, University of Utah, Salt Lake City – U.S.A.
Professor George Tesar, Umeå University, Umeå – Sweden
Professor José de la Torre, Florida International University, Miami – U.S.A.
Professor Rosalie L. Tung, Simon Fraser University, Burnaby, BC – Canada
Professor Jean-Claude Usunier, University of Lousanne, Lousanne – Dorigny – Switzerland
Professor Alain Charles Verbeke, Vrije Universiteit Brussel – Belgium
Professor Lawrence S. Welch, Mt Eliza Business School, Melbourne, Australia
Professor Martin K. Welge, Universität Dortmund – Germany
Professor Bernard Yin Yeung, New York University – U.S.A.
Professor Masaru Yoshimori, Yokohama National University – Japan

BOOK REVIEW EDITOR

Professor Dr. Johann Engelhard, Universität Bamberg – Germany

EDITOR

MANAGEMENT INTERNATIONAL REVIEW, *Professor Dr. Profs. h.c. Dr. h.c. Klaus Macharzina, Universität Hohenheim (510 E), Schloss-Osthof-Ost, D-70599 Stuttgart, Germany, Tel. (0711) 459-29 08, Fax (0711) 459-32 88, E-mail: klausmac@uni-hohenheim.de, Internet: http://www.uni-hohenheim.de/~mir Assistant Editors: Professor Dr. Michael-Jörg Oesterle, Universität Bremen, Germany, Professor Dr. Joachim Wolf, Universität Kiel, Germany, Editorial office: Mrs. Sylvia Ludwig*

Management
International Review
© Gabler Verlag 2003

VOLUME 43 · SPECIAL ISSUE · 2003/2

CONTENTS

Guest Editor's Introduction 3
Manuel Becerra/Juan Santaló
An Empirical Analysis of the Corporate Effect: The Impact of the Multinational Corporation on the Performance of Its Units Worldwide 7
Alfredo J. Mauri/Rakesh B. Sambharya
The Performance Implications of a Global Integration Strategy in Global Industries: An Empirical Investigation Using Inter-area Product Flows 27
Niels G. Noorderhaven/Anne-Wil Harzing
The "Country-of-origin Effect" in Multinational Corporations: Sources, Mechanisms and Moderating Conditions 47
Peter J. Buckley/Jeremy Clegg/Hui Tan
The Art of Knowledge Transfer: Secondary and Reverse Transfer in China's Telecommunications Manufacturing Industry 67
Fiona Moore
Internal Diversity and Culture's Consequences: Branch/Head Office Relations in a German Financial MNC 95

GUIDELINE FOR AUTHORS

mir welcomes articles on original theoretical contributions, empirical research, state-of-the-art surveys or reports on recent developments in the areas of

a) International Business b) Transnational Corporations c) Intercultural Management d) Strategic Management e) Business Policy.

Manuscripts are reviewed with the understanding that they are substantially new, have not been previously published in whole (including book chapters) or in part (including exhibits), have not been previously accepted for publication, are not under consideration by any other publisher, and will not be submitted elsewhere until a decision is reached regarding their publication in mir. The only exception is papers in conference proceedings, which we treat as work-in-progress.

Contributions should be submitted in English language in a Microsoft or compatible format by e-mail to the Editor at klausmac@uni-hohenheim.de. The complete text including the references, tables and figures should as a rule not exceed 25 pages in a usual setting (approximately *7000 words*). Reply papers should normally not exceed 1500 words. The title page should include the following elements: Author(s) name, Heading of the article, Abstract (two sections of about 30 words each), Key Results (20 words), Author's line (author's name, academic title, position and affiliation) and on the bottom a proposal for an abbreviated heading on the front cover of the journal.

Submitted papers must be written according to mir's formal guidelines. Only those manuscripts can enter the reviewing process which adhere to our guidelines. Authors are requested to

- use *endnotes* for clarification sparingly. References to the literature are indicated in the text by author's name and year of publication in parentheses, e.g. (Reitsperger/Daniel 1990, p. 210, Eiteman 1989). The references should be listed in alphabetical order at the end of the text. They should include full bibliographical details and be cited in the following manner: e.g.

    Reitsperger, W. D./Daniel, S. J., Dynamic Manufacturing: A Comparison of Attitudes in the U.S. and Japan, *Management International Review*, 30, 1990, pp. 203–216.

    Eiteman, D. K., Financial Sourcing, in Macharzina, K./Welge, M. K. (eds.), *Handwörterbuch Export und Internationale Unternehmung*, Stuttgart: Poeschel 1989, pp. 602–621.

    Stopford, J. M./Wells, L. T. Jr., *Managing the Multinational Enterprise*, New York: Basic Books 1972.

- avoid *terms* that may be interpreted denigrating to ethnic or other groups.
- be especially careful in dealing with gender. Traditional customs such as "... the manager wishes that **his** interest ..." can favor the acceptance of inequality were none exist. The use of plural pronouns is preferred. If this is impossible, the term "he or she" or "he/she" can be used.

In the case of publication authors are supplied one complimentary copy of the issue and 30 off-prints free of charge. Additional copies may be ordered *prior to printing*. Overseas shipment is by boat; air-delivery will be charged extra.

The author agrees, that his/her article is published not only in this journal but that it can also be reproduced by the publisher and his licensees through license agreement in other journals (also in translated versions), through reprint in omnibus volumes (i.e. for anniversary editions of the journal or the publisher or in subject volumes), through longer extracts in books of the publisher also for advertising purposes, through multiplication and distribution on CD ROM.or other data media, through storage on data bases, their transmission and retrieval, during the time span of the copyright laws on the article at home and abroad.

Management
International Review
© Gabler Verlag 2003

Guest Editor's Introduction

Multinational corporations (MNCs) are frequently pictured as being at the vanguard of global integration. MNCs face strong incentives to maximize economies of scale in research and development, purchasing, production and marketing, and encounter low barriers in the dissemination of technologies and best practices. The days are past that subsidiaries of MNCs operated as quasi-independent companies, optimally adapted to local circumstances and with very little interference from headquarters. Even in markets where adaptation to local circumstances is mandatory, MNCs work hard to bridge the gap between global and local, and to identify ways of reconciling global integration, e.g., in production, with the required extent of local responsiveness, e.g., in marketing

Thus, MNCs function as motors of a process of international convergence that may ultimately make national differences rooted in institutional and cultural idiosyncracies less relevant or may even make these differences disappear. However, very few studies have empirically gauged processes of global integration in MNCs. Those studies that *did* seek to investigate global integration within MNCs found that in addition to convergence due to company-wide policies there are also enduring sources of divergence, such as attempts by local subsidiaries to become centers of excellence (Bélanger et al. 1999). Furthermore, there are also studies demonstrating that cultural and institutional differences play a role in the manner in which seemingly universal techniques and procedures are implemented within different countries (Hancké/Casper 2000).

This special issue of *Management International Review* brings together five papers that focus on different aspects of the tension between global and local within MNCs, and the attempts of MNCs to integrate internationally in spite of these tensions. In the first paper, Becerra and Santaló study the question to what extent being a part of a particular MNC influences the performance of regional units. This can be seen as an indicator of the extent to which the MNC is capable of putting its corporate-level resources to work on a global scale. Becerra and Santaló find that about ten percent of the variability of regional units is attributable to corporate effects. The more internationalized the MNC is, the stronger the corporate effect. This suggests that the more internationalized MNCs are also more successful in integrating their international operations, whether by employing worldwide home-grown advantages, or by spreading over the entire organization resources and capabilities developed by a particular subsidiary.

This integration within the MNC, that can be assumed to be responsible for the stronger corporate effect in the more internationalized MNCs in Becerra and Santaló's sample, is the focus of Mauri and Sambharya's paper. These authors study the effect of global integration on the performance of the MNC, operationalizing global integration as the inter-area product flows within the multinational. They find a non-linear relation between global integration and MNC performance. At low levels of global integration, there is a negative relation with performance, which turns positive at intermediate levels, but negative again at very high levels of global integration. Their explanation is that at very low and very high levels of integration the balance between the costs and benefits of global integration activities is negative. At low levels this is because of the high setup costs of international integrative devices, at very high levels the boundaries of effectively managing of a network of specialized and geographically dispersed subsidiaries are reached. Only at intermediate levels global integration yields surplus value.

In the third paper Noorderhaven and Harzing focus on an issue somewhat related to that of both previous papers, but from a very different angle. MNCs not only influence the performance of their subsidiaries and the entire organization through the integration and transfer of resources and capabilities, they also exert a homogenizing influence through company-wide management approaches and control systems. These management approaches and control strategies, in turn, are heavily influenced by the national origin of the MNC. This influence cannot easily be described in the global versus local terminology, it is a dominance of certain local approaches over others. In Noorderhaven and Harzing's paper the sources of these country-of-origin effects in MNCs are discussed, and propositions are formulated concerning the home-country and MNC-related conditions that moderate their strength.

Buckley, Clegg and Tan look more closely at the processes of knowledge transfer within MNCs that so often are taken for granted. Focusing on two firms in the telecommunication sector in China, the processes of knowledge transfer between these firms and their western parent companies, as well as between these firms and other subsidiaries of the same parent firms are studied. Their findings demonstrate path-dependency: the ownership entry strategy of the western parent firm locks their Chinese subsidiary or joint venture into constraints from which it is difficult to escape. Buckley, Clegg and Tan's findings and analysis show that MNCs cannot choose freely in their integration strategies, in as far as knowledge transfer is concerned, as they are constrained by previously made, seemingly unrelated choices.

The paper by Moore, finally, looks more closely at MNC integration strategy, in her case that of a German multinational bank as it is received at its London branch. Her observations give yet another turn to the local-global dichotomy. Not only are the integrative pressures exerted by head office embedded in a highly local perspective on the business (putting their 'global' character in doubt), but the responses at the London branch diverge between local sub-groups. This case study shows that it is not only too simplistic to think in terms of local-global dichotomies, it is even too simplistic to think in terms of confrontation between localities, as the identities within MNCs transgress the boundaries of local units. MNCs that ignore these diverse identities at localities do so at their peril, as Moore's case study illustrates.

Taken together the five papers in this special issue drive home both the importance and the complexity of international integration within MNCs. International integration in multinationals is important, as it is related to the performance of the MNC (Becerra and Santaló; Mauri and Sambharya). However, this integration does not necessarily make the MNC a harbinger of best practices, as the influence of headquarters may be more like the dominance of one particular local approach over others (Noorderhaven and Harzing). As far as the transfer of technology is concerned, the capabilities of MNCs to perform this effectively critically depend on other corporate strategies and management practices, with the effect that a company may get locked into a trajectory that seriously hinders further integration of competences and capabilities (Buckley, Clegg and Tan). Finally, international integration within MNCs is best pictured not as the substitution of global for local practices, nor as an opposition between competing local approaches, but as a process in which practices are shared and transferred smoothly among certain groups within the MNC, cutting through the boundaries of organizational units, but not in others (Moore). All in all, these papers suggest that it is time to leave behind thinking of MNCs in terms of 'local' and 'global', and to come to grips with the much more complicated reality these organizations have to deal with.

NIELS G. NOORDERHAVEN

References

Bélanger, J./Berggren, C./Bjorkman, T./Kohler, C. (eds.), *Being Local Worldwide: ABB and the Challenge of Global Management*. Ithaca, NY: Cornell University Press 1999.

Hancké, B./Casper, S., Reproducing diversity; ISO 9000 and work organisation in the French and German car industry. In S. Quack, G. Morgan and R. Whitley, (eds.), *National Capitalisms, Global Competition, and Economic Performance*. Amsterdam: John Benjamins, 2000, pp. 173–188.

Management International Review

Neuerscheinungen

Doris Lindner
**Einflussfaktoren
des erfolgreichen
Auslandseinsatzes**
Konzeptionelle Grundlagen –
Bestimmungsgrößen – Ansatzpunkte
zur Verbesserung
2002
XX, 341 S. mit 38 Abb., 21 Tab.,
(mir-Edition),
Br. € 59,–
ISBN 3-409-11952-3

Tobias Specker
**Postmerger-Management in den
ost- und mitteleuropäischen
Transformationsstaaten**
2002
XX, 431 S. mit 60 Abb., 28 Tab.,
(mir-Edition),
Br. € 64,–
ISBN 3-409-12010-6

Jörg Frehse
**Internationale
Dienstleistungskompetenzen**
Erfolgsstrategien für die europäische
Hotellerie
2002
XXVI, 353 S. mit 48 Abb.,
(mir-Edition),
Br. € 59,–
ISBN 3-409-12349-0

Anja Schulte
**Das Phänomen
der Rückverlagerung**
Internationale Standortent-
scheidungen kleiner und mittlerer
Unternehmen
2002
XXII, 315 S. mit 17 Abb., 2 Tab.,
(mir-Edition),
Br. € 59,–
ISBN 3-409-12375-X

Andreas Wald
**Netzwerkstrukturen und
-effekte in Organisationen**
Eine Netzwerkanalyse
in internationalen Unternehmen
2003
XVIII, 238 S. mit 19 Abb., 61 Tab.,
(mir-Edition),
Br. € 49,90
ISBN 3-409-12395-4

Nicola Berg
Public Affairs Management
Ergebnisse einer empirischen
Untersuchung in Multinationalen
Unternehmungen
2003
XXXIV, 471 S. mit 20 Abb., 67 Tab.
(mir-Edition),
Br. € 64,–
ISBN 3-409-12387-3

Betriebswirtschaftlicher Verlag Dr. Th. Gabler GmbH, Abraham-Lincoln-Str. 46, 65189 Wiesbaden

Manuel Becerra/Juan Santaló

An Empirical Analysis of the Corporate Effect: The Impact of the Multinational Corporation on the Performance of Its Units Worldwide[1]

Abstract

- This paper investigates the sources of variability of MNC performance in different areas of the world, particularly the influence of corporate-level factors, the geographical areas, and their specific industries.

- The key goal is to measure to what extent MNC corporate-level resources, such as ownership advantages and core competencies, affect the performance of the MNC's international subsidiaries.

Key Results

- Variance decomposition analysis shows that approximately 10% of the performance of MNCs in different parts of world can be attributed to the corporation as a whole. As expected, this corporate effect is larger for more highly internationalized firms.

Authors

Manuel Becerra, Professor of Strategy and International Management, Instituto de Empresa, Madrid, Spain.
Juan Santaló, Professor of Strategy, Instituto de Empresa, Madrid, Spain.

Introduction

The literature on international diversification and performance constitutes one of the central topics in the field of international business (Hitt/Hoskisson/Kim 1997, Dess et al. 1995). Researchers have suggested a number of reasons why multinational corporations may enjoy a significant advantage over their less internationalized competitors, such as greater market opportunities (Buhner 1987), benefits from internalization and integration (Rugman 1981, Kobrin 1991), increased market power and lower risk (Kim/Hwang/Burgers 1989), greater opportunities for learning (Kogut 1984), and many other arguments generally related to acquiring "ownership advantages" and exploiting them in different locations (Dunning 1988, Delios/Beamish 1999).

The mixed empirical evidence points toward some positive relationship between international scope and performance (Kim/Hwang/ Burgers 1989), probably curvilinear (Hitt et al. 1997), and moderated by the extent of product diversification (Hitt et al. 1997, Delios/Beamish 1999), which would explain the insignificant results obtained in some studies (Geringer/Beamish/daCosta 1989). This research has been criticized for being often descriptive rather than analyzing why we observe certain empirical association (Dess et al. 1995). More recently, however, researchers are probing further into what lies behind the performance implications of international diversification and, for instance, whether greater performance results from greater geographical scope or vice versa (Delios/Beamish 1999).

This paper is aimed at expanding this line of research from a different angle. Rather than explaining the direct impact of international diversification on MNC performance, we will study the sources of variability of MNC performance worldwide, particularly its corporate-level resources and the moderating role of international diversification. The focus is, thus, placed on the relative importance of the different factors that drive the performance of MNCs throughout the world, i.e. how global is indeed the performance of MNCs throughout their different local units. The key research questions to be investigated are: How much, if anything, of the performance of a MNC in different regions of the world is attributable to the corporation as a whole? How does the degree of internationalization affect the size of this corporate effect?

As mentioned above, the abundant empirical research on the international diversification-performance relationship is based on the assumption that ownership advantages drive the performance of the MNC and that greater unique advantages of the MNC should be empirically observable in the higher performance of more internationalized firms. The empirical studies of this stream of research try to estimate this relationship between internationalization and performance through a regression coefficient. In contrast, this paper does not study the direct relationship between internationalization and MNC performance, but instead it investigates the relative influence of the entire MNC versus other factors that presumably explain the performance of MNCs across their lower-level units worldwide. In addition, we will also study whether this influence is moderated by the extent of internationalization of the MNCs.

The methodology and underlying motivation of this paper draws heavily from recent research on strategic management that investigates the sources of variance of firm performance and, particularly, the relative effects of the industry, the corporation, and the product-based business unit in diversified companies (Rumelt 1991, McGahan/Porter 1997). The study brings this research approach into the international arena, where the focus is now on the performance of the MNC across different geographical areas and, mainly, the corporate effect in multinationals. Thus, whereas earlier research focuses on the corporate effect of diversified firms across their different product-based subsidiaries, we will study the corporate effect of internationalized firms across their different geographic-based subsidiaries. Such a MNC corporate effect (as opposed to the product-based corporate effect in diversified corporations investigated in earlier research in strategy) plays an important implicit role in the theory of International Business that has not been empirically investigated and measured yet. A significant MNC corporate effect would provide justification for the study of corporate strategy in MNCs and, more specifically, the role of the corporate office and other corporate-level factors that affect the performance of the MNC worldwide.

The next section discusses the results from previous research in the field of strategy that explore the corporate effect in diversified corporations. Later, this notion is extended to the international context of MNCs where the effect of corporation as whole is investigated over its different regional units, rather than over its product-based divisions explored in earlier research. The following sections present the methodology used in the study and the conclusions regarding the effect of corporate-level factors on the performance of MNCs in different regions worldwide. We conclude the paper with a discussion of the meaning of the corporate effect for MNCs, the different types of influence that the MNC headquarters can provide, and the limitations and implications of the findings for the field of international business.

The Corporate Effect

The Corporate Effect for Diversified Firms

For about a decade, scholars in the fields of Strategy and Industrial Organization have engaged in a debate about the relative importance of different sources of organizational performance (Schmalensee 1985, Hansen/Wernerfelt 1989, Rumelt 1991, Powell 1996, Roquebert/Phillips/Westfall 1996, McGahan/Porter 1997). Using several methods of variance decomposition, these researchers have estimated how much of the performance of the business units in their samples (with responsibilities for a given line of products or services within larger diversified corporations) can be attributed to: (1) the industry in which the units compete, (2) the corporation to which they belong, (3) unit-specific factors stable through time, and (4) other factors and random variations in business unit performance (error term).

Using typically a set of dummy variables that reflect the industry, the corporation, and the period in which the performance of a business unit was observed (usually ROA), a components of variance analysis would estimate how much of the performance in relative terms is attributable to the industry, the corporation, and the business. Despite some differences in methodologies and datasets, the results of this line of research are starting to converge into a somewhat coherent picture of sources of organizational performance. Industry membership seems to be an important factor that accounts for an average of almost 20% of business-unit performance. This result, first obtained by Schmalensee (1985), highlights the relevance of the industry and the competitive context in which firms operate. On the other hand, business-unit specific factors stable through time account for nearly 40% of business-unit performance (Rumelt 1991, Roquebert et al. 1996). Thus, business-level considerations seem to be twice as important as industry-level influences in explaining organizational performance (Rumelt 1991, Hansen/Wernerfelt 1989, Powell 1996). This result provides empirical support for the claim that firm strategies should be studied beyond the analysis of industry structure and attractiveness (Rumelt 1991).

The corporate effect has been more difficult to detect empirically. Schmalensee (1985) and Rumelt (1991) showed their surprise to find only a negligible impact of corporations over their business units using data from the FTC database in manufacturing industries. More recently, other researchers have detected a larger corporate effect using different approaches (Roquebert et al. 1996, McGahan/Porter 1997, Brush/Bromiley/Hendrickx 1999).

As it is measured and tested in these studies, a negligible corporate effect in this sample of diversified firms would mean that the performance of a corporation's business units in different industries is not due to corporate-level factors.

Several researchers have claimed that, therefore, this result would imply that corporate strategy would not matter (Bowman/Helfat 2001) and that we should focus on business-level competitive strategy. In such case, studying the corporate office, the decisions they take, and the resources that affect the entire corporation (i.e., all the business units across the corporation) would be useless, since performance would be mostly determined at the business unit level.

The corporate effect detected by more recent empirical research provides evidence, however, that indeed the corporate office and corporate-level resources in general have an impact on the performance of its lower-level business units, either creating or destroying value through the corporate management of the diversified firm. For instance, diversified companies may be able to benefit from vertical, synergistic, and financial economies generated by having different businesses under the same corporate umbrella (Hill/Hoskisson 1987); as a result, firms, whose corporate office does a better job in taking advantage of these possibilities, would have better performance. It is the role of the corporate office to make sure that these economies are realized through their administrative (loss prevention) and entrepreneurial (value-creation) activities throughout the entire organization (Chandler 1991).

The Corporate Effect in MNCs

The previous discussion and the existing empirical research have dealt exclusively with the effect of corporate-level resources on diversified firms. In addition to product diversification, however, the corporate office, wherever it may be located, also manages geographical diversification. In MNCs, their headquarters, regional offices, and centers of excellence have the responsibility to integrate the activities of the organization worldwide. The impact of corporate-level resources on the international operations and performance of the MNC worldwide constitutes the essence of the ownership advantages that lie behind the nature of the MNC, particularly the generation and the transfer of competitive advantage and knowledge across borders (Dunning 1988, Bartlett/Ghoshal 1989).

MNCs need to develop operational capabilities to manage interdependencies and various resource flows through the MNC network (Roth/Schweiger/Morrison 1991). These capabilities include, for instance, the coordination and configuration of the functional activities worldwide (Porter 1986) and the managerial philosophy shared throughout the MNC (Bartlett/Ghoshal 1989). There is a vast literature that analyzes the different control and coordination activities of the MNC corporate office and the change in its role toward more subtle coordination mechanisms (Doz/Prahalad 1981, Martinez/Jarillo 1989, Ferlie/Pettigrew 1996). The coordination of subsidiaries can be a source of value for the MNC (Kogut 1985). For instance, Nohria and Ghoshal (1994) have shown that MNCs can improve their performance by adapting their headquarters-subsidiary relationships to fit.

In an international business context, corporate-level decisions and competencies, like the ability to coordinate the activities among geographically dispersed units, can have a direct impact on the performance of the subsidiaries worldwide. In fact, the units of the MNC depend on the corporation as a whole for key human, financial, technological, and managerial resources and for coordination activities (Doz/Prahalad 1981). These resources that reside at the corporate level and are used throughout the MNC should impact all the international subsidiaries and their performance in local markets. Such an impact should be empirically detectable as a corporate effect that would reflect to what extent there are MNC-level factors behind the performance of lower-level geographical units (e.g., MNC ownership advantages). In this paper, we want to measure how large is this MNC corporate effect relative to other factors that may drive the performance of MNCs, such as industry influences.

Extent of Internationalization and the Size of the Corporate Effect

The argument above deals with the presumed impact of various corporate-level factors on the international subsidiaries of the MNC. We could expect this influence to be larger when the MNC has more or better corporate-level resources to share across or transfer to its subsidiaries. When properly managed, the corporate office facilitates the realization of the economies from internationalization through activities of control and coordination within the MNC (Doz/Prahalad 1981). These activities have an impact on the performance of each of their international subsidiaries and, through aggregation, in the entire MNC. It is reasonable to believe that more internationalized MNCs can take greater advantage of the economies of scale, scope, and learning that having international presence provides by standardizing products, rationalizing production, and coordinating critical resources (Kogut 1985, Kobrin 1991), thus showing a greater corporate effect in the performance of their different units worldwide.

The possibilities for global learning of more internationalized MNCs have been stressed, in particular, by Bartlett and Ghoshal (1989). Transnational corporations, with dispersed and interdependent assets and resources embodied in subsidiaries with specialized roles, have the opportunity to learn from different locations and transfer the accumulated knowledge to other subsidiaries within the organization that may need it (Bartlett/Ghoshal 1989, Hitt/Cheng 2002, Doz/Santos/Williamson 2001). Corporate MNC headquarters have an important role in facilitating this learning of the subsidiary and the entire MNC (Doz/Santos/Williamson 2001), which may be expected to be greater when the MNC is more internationalized.

This idea is also consistent with traditional internalization theory (Rugman 1981, Dunning 1988). MNCs with a larger international presence may take advantage of globalization and worldwide learning to build a competitive advantage for the entire MNC (Rugman 1981, Doz/Santos/Williamson 2001). Assuming that ownership advantages allow firms to become MNCs in the first place (Hymer 1960, Dunning 1988), those MNCs with larger ownership advantages can be expected to become more highly internationalized. In this case, we should also observe a greater corporate effect for more internationalized MNCs, though the driving force would be the initial amount of corporate-level resources and advantages that started off the process of internationalization. It should be noted that this paper is not aimed at clarifying the causality direction between extent of internationalization and an MNC's corporate-level factors, but the empirical analysis of the MNC corporate effect and how it relates to the extent of MNC internationalization.

Finally, a positive relation between the size of the corporate effect and the extent of internationalization is also consistent with the abundant empirical literature that has detected a positive relationship between degree of internationalization and MNC performance (Buhner 1987, Kim/Kwang/Burgers 1989, Rugman 1979). However, a corporate effect would also be detectable with any other relationship, whether linear or not, such as a quadratic relationship (Hitt/Hoskisson/Kim 1997) and even a negative association (Geringer/Beamish/daCosta 1989). The key idea is not whether international diversification provides an intrinsic advantage or disadvantage to the MNC, like Grant, Jammine, and Thomas (1988) claim, or, based on the opposite causality relationship, whether the internationalization results from the amount of ownership advantages available to the MNC. Instead, our goal is to measure whether more internationalized MNCs have a larger corporate effect relative to other factors that could presumably drive the performance of MNC in different geographical areas worldwide.

The arguments supporting the notion of a detectable MNC corporate effect on its lower-level units is already implicit in the existing literature in strategy and international business, but it has not been measured in terms of relative impact, nor has been estimated for different levels of internationalization. In the next section, we will discuss different ways to estimate this effect as well as the sample of MNCs used in the study.

Methodology

Data

To investigate empirically the MNC corporate effect, we used data from Compustat. This database compiles information about publicly held companies from the Securities and Exchange Commission and other sources, such as the stock market and accounting statements of the corporations. As opposed to Roquebert et al. (1996) and McGahan and Porter (1997), who used the Compustat Business Segment Reports, this study is based on the Geographic Segment Reports that provide information about the subsidiaries performance in different countries or regions in the world.

To base the analysis on a relatively homogeneous set of highly internationalized firms and to reduce other potential sources of variability not controlled for, we focused on the 100 largest American corporations from the 1994 Standard and Poor's list. Though every company in the S&P100 reported data for their US operations, there was wide variation in the denomination of their other international operations, usually one or two countries per continent and occasionally the continent itself. We aggregated these international operations to the continent level to reduce empty cells in the design and to allow meaningful comparisons. Therefore, the unit of analysis is (called regional unit in this paper) the MNC in each of four regions worldwide (North America, Europe, Asia-Pacific, and South America).

We collected annual data on Net Income and Identifiable Assets from 1991 to 1994 for each regional unit to compute the Return on Assets (ROA), which is the performance measure traditionally used in research on sources of performance (Rumelt 1991, McGahan/Porter 1997). To determine each MNC's industry, we used the 4-digit primary-SIC code in which the MNC (and also each of its regional units) competed.

From this initial sample, we placed several constraints on the firms and the industries in the sample to eliminate single-unit cells, so that the different effects could be distinguished for all observations. Thus, we eliminated firms that were present in only one geographical area and also those industries that did not have at least two MNCs in the sample. If we had not included these constraints, it would not have been possible to separate the area, the corporate, and the regional unit effects for the observations in the first case, and the industry and the corporate effect in the second case. Finally, we deleted four clear outliers with extremely high ROA greater than 100%, substantially above the rest of the observations.

The final dataset had 747 observations, which represent 76 American MNCs in 14 industries, 4 geographic areas, and data for 4 years for the 198 regional units in the sample. Following standard practice in this stream of literature, we used dummy codes to capture how much of the variability in ROA in the sample can be attributed to the different year, industries, corporations, geographical areas, and lower-level units within the MNC (regional units). Therefore, each observation contains the dependent variable (ROA of the regional unit) and a set of dummy codes: year (4), industry (14), corporation (76), area (4), and regional unit (198). The characteristics of the sample result in a complex research design in which corporation is nested within industry, and regional unit is nested within corporation, industry, and area. Descriptive statistics for the sample are shown in Table 1.

Table 1. Descriptive Statistics

1. – Sample Characteristics
198 Regional units for 4 years, 747 total observations in:
- 76 US MNCs
- 4 geographical areas
- 14 industries

2. – Average Profitability:

* By Period	ROA	Regional units	MNCs	
1. Year 1991	0.1500	180	75	
2. Year 1992	0.1142	185	75	
3. Year 1993	0.1319	190	75	
4. Year 1994	0.1102	192	75	
For Periods 1–4 (total sample)	0.1263	747	76	
* By Area				
1. US	0.1198	292	74	
2. South America	0.1469	73	21	
3. Europe	0.1018	220	59	
4. Asia-Pacific	0.1621	162	44	
* By Industry				Foreign Assets to Total Assets
1. SIC 1311 Energy	0.0751	41	4	22.25%
2. SIC 2000 Food	0.1640	37	4	24.72%
3. SIC 2040 Processed Foods	0.1540	44	4	32.27%
4. SIC 2621 Paper	0.0649	38	5	30.02%
5. SIC 2800 Chemical	0.1116	52	5	25.07%
6. SIC 2834 Pharmaceutical	0.2692	112	11	27.78%
7. SIC 2911 Oil	0.0603	92	11	23.41%
8. SIC 3510 Engines and Turbines	0.0537	34	4	20.85%
9. SIC 3570 Computers	0.0447	60	5	42.20%
10. SIC 3571 Microcomputers	0.1147	79	8	29.34%
11. SIC 3711 Automobiles	0.0319	32	3	18.50%
12. SIC 3714 Motor Vehicle Parts	0.0984	42	4	25.76%
13. SIC 3841 Medical Instruments	0.1750	40	4	30.30%
14. SIC 7372 Software	0.1985	44	4	53.72%

Estimation

We used two different methods to decompose the observed variability in regional unit ROA into the five independent variables under study (i.e., sources of performance): year, industry, corporation, area, and regional unit effects.

The different effects can be estimated through hierarchical regression analysis in which the independent variables are added in a sequence of steps. The increase in R^2 of the last set of dummy variables indicates the relevance of such an effect. A test of significance can be performed for each step and the increase in R^2 for each one measures the relative effect of each source of performance. Unfortunately, since regional areas are nested within corporations, we cannot regress regional areas first and then the corporate dummies, because the regional areas would capture all the variability. However, if we regress corporations first and then the regional areas, we could not be sure that the variability absorbed by the corporate dummy variables is not really due to lower level variability in regional areas (Rumelt 1991). Thus, hierarchical OLS regression (fixed-effects ANOVA) should be interpreted with caution only as a maximum possible estimate for the corporate effect (Bowman/Helfat 1998).

An alternative methodology widely used in previous research is the variance components approach (Schmalensee 1985, Rumelt 1991, Roquebert et al. 1996, McGahan/Porter 1997). This method has several advantages over the fixed-effect hierarchical regression. We can estimate the relative importance of the diverse effects simultaneously, despite the nesting of the model, and therefore we can now distinguish the corporate from the regional unit effect. Furthermore, this methodology allows a much more efficient use of degrees of freedom, since only five parameters need to be estimated, i.e., the variances for each effect[2]. When using this approach, we assume that all effects are realizations of random processes, with zero means and constant but unknown variances, from an underlying population of the class of effects.

In the next section, we estimate the different effects using these two alternative methods. Though the actual estimates are expected to differ across methods, a large corporate effect in both would lend support for the importance of corporate-level resources in the MNC. Given the emphasis on the measurement of the corporate effect in this paper, we consider appropriate to present the results from these two alternative methods to observe the robustness of the results across methodologies[3].

Results

For the traditional fixed-effects hierarchical regression analysis (OLS), we introduced the sets of dummy variables in the following order: period, area, industry, corporate, and regional unit. The full model shown in Table 2 provides an adjusted R^2 of 0.70. When we include the corporate dummy variables in the model, the R^2 increases by 0.24 (significant at 0.001 level), providing initial evidence in favor of a significant corporate effect. This figure is larger than Rumelt's (1991) and McGahan and Porter's (1997) estimates of 0.15 and 0.09 respectively. However, as discussed in the previous section, we have to interpret this estimate with caution, only as the maximum possible magnitude of the actual corporate effect in MNCs.

In Table 3, we present the components of variance computed from the Expected Mean Square estimates obtained from the GLM procedure in SAS, when all effects are considered random in this nested design. We also report the estimates of McGahan and Porter (1997), Roquebert et al. (1996), Rumelt (1991), and Schmalensee (1985).

The 17.90% industry effect we find is similar to the ones that these studies report that oscillates near 20%. More important for this paper, we can see that 10% of the variability in the performance of the regional units in our study is attributable to corporate effects. This statistically significant result is larger than the 4.3% corporate effect for the business units of domestic corporations obtained by McGahan and Porter (1997) or the negligible effect found by Rumelt (1991) and Schamlensee (1985); however, it is substantially smaller than the 17.9%

Table 2. Fixed-Effects Hierarchical Regressions

Effects	df	Increase in R^2	F value
Period	3	0.01	2.381*
Area	3	0.02	5.155***
Industry	13	0.21	15.083***
Corporate	62	0.24	4.912***
Regional unit	119	0.31	6.445***
Total Model	200	0.78	9.796***
Error	546	0.22	
Adjusted R^2		0.71	

NOTE: Each variable is included in a sequence of steps that incorporate the previous variables. The F value is computed for the last variable included in the model in this set of sequential regression analyses.

* significant at 0.1 level
** significant at 0.05 level
*** significant at 0.01 level

reported by Roquebert et al. (1996) for their full sample results (which decreased to about 5% when the less diversified corporations were excluded). Our estimation of the regional unit effect, 40.88%, is larger than the 31% business unit effect found by McGahan and Porter, but lower than the 46% reported by Rumelt. Thus, the analysis of variance for the full sample provided clear evidence in favor of a MNC corporate effect for the full sample.

It should be noted that we also replicated the analysis using just a cross-section of the data to check whether the inclusion of data from several years could be affecting the results. Each observation in this cross-section contained the average of ROA for the four-year period, as well as the different sets of dummies. In this analysis, we found very similar estimates, in fact a greater corporate effect, to the ones we report in the paper for the full sample.

Next, we investigated how the extent of internationalization affects the size of the corporate effect. For each MNC, we constructed the ratio foreign assets to total assets with information reported in Compustat. We use this ratio as a proxy for the degree of internationalization of the company in order to divide the full sample into three equal-sized parts. One sub-sample contains the 33% of observations that belong to relatively low-internationalized companies in which the MNCs had an internationalization ratio below .25. Another sub-sample has the 33% of observations corresponding to relatively medium-internationalized companies, while the last sub-sample includes the 33% of observation from highly-internationalized corporations with a ratio larger than .32. We show the results of the subsample analysis in Table 4.

We expected that the corporate effect should be larger for more internationalized MNCs and the estimates of the variance components show this hypothesis to be correct. The results reported in Table 4 indicate that the corporate effect is indeed more important for the highly internationalized MNCs (19%) than both in the medium internationalized (11%) and the less internationalized MNCs (0%). It seems that the relevance of the corporate effect increases linearly with the degree

Table 3. Variance Components Estimates (%)

Source	This study	Roquebert et alia (1996)	McGahan/ Porter (1997)	Rumelt (1991)	Schmalensee (1985)
Period	1.06	2.3	2.39	0	x
Area	2.15	x	x	x	x
Industry	17.90	10.2	18.68	16.12	19.46
Corporate	9.99	17.9	4.33	0.80	0
Regional unit	40.88	–	–	–	–
(Business unit)	–	37.1	31.71	46.38	x
Error	27.99	32.0	48.40	36.70	80.54

x indicates that the variance for that effect was not estimated

Table 4. Variance Components Estimates by Degree of Internationalization (%)

Source	Full Sample	Low Internat. Sub-sample	Medium Internat. Sub-sample	High Internat. Sub-sample
Period	1.06	0.31	5.66**	1.89
Area	2.15*	4.30	10.29***	0.53
Industry	17.90***	45.56***	19.89***	0
Corporate	9.99**	0	10.84	18.99*
Regional unit (Business unit)	40.88***	32.91***	22.34**	46.97***
Error	27.99	16.89	30.94	31.60

* significant at 0.1 level
** significant at 0.05 level
*** significant at 0.01 level

of internationalization of the MNC, while the effect of the industry decreases. The corporate effect is not significant in either the low or medium internationalized firms, but it is at least marginally significant (p-value of 5.6%) for the most internationalized companies. We believe that the low number of observations in each sub-sample makes it very difficult to find high levels of statistical significance[4].

Discussion

This study expands to an international context the investigation on sources of organizational performance. Whereas strategy researchers have studied the corporate effect in diversified corporations in the US, this paper investigates the influence of corporate-level factors on the performance of the regional units of MNCs worldwide. Based on variance decomposition analysis, the results show that a significant corporate effect can be detected for a sample of some of the largest American MNCs. This effect accounts for approximately 10% of their performance in different regions of the world. Though the factors behind this corporate effect are not explicitly analyzed in this paper, they are widely used in the strategy and international business literature (e.g., core competencies and ownership advantages). Therefore, the empirical support obtained in this paper provides evidence in favor of the study of corporate-level issues in MNCs, in particular the role of the corporate office.

Measuring the MNC Corporate Effect

Since, to our knowledge, this is the first paper to estimate the corporate effect in MNCs, it is worthwhile to discuss what exactly is being measured. The variance decomposition methodology that we employed measures in relative terms the extent to which the variability in performance of the MNCs across different regions of the world can be attributed to the whole MNC worldwide, as opposed to other sources of performance like the specific industry of the MNC, the area in which the regional unit operates, the year when the measure is taken, and other stable-through-time factors associated with the regional unit of the MNC. Since the corporate effect is measured through a dummy variable that identifies the different MNCs in the sample, it actually estimates the portion of the performance of the regional units that is shared with other units of the same MNC. Therefore, it includes any direct impact of the MNC corporate office (that all international subsidiaries feel to a similar extent), but also any other tangible or intangible resources of the MNC as a whole that potentially affect the performance of subsidiaries worldwide. Thus, it basically absorbs any overlap in performance, positive or negative, of the different regional units of the MNCs in the sample. It is, therefore, an average estimate of how much of the variability in performance of regional units can be attributed to corporate-level factors, though in each MNC the corporate effect will be greater or smaller than the 10% estimate for the entire sample.

This shared overlap is associated with the ability of the corporate office to directly influence the units or transfer among them capabilities and advantages developed locally. However, there are different ways in which we could obtain a corporate effect for the MNC. In our opinion, we could think of the corporate effect as comprised by three elements based on where it originated initially: the corporate office, the entire corporation, or specific subsidiaries. First, the source of the advantage could be located precisely at the corporate office. MNC headquarters, with its practices and decisions, provide guidance to the organization and, thus, affects positively or negatively its subsidiaries (Ferlie/Pettigrew 1996). Second, the strategic resource may actually reside in all the regional subsidiaries at once, through the effect of some "ownership" advantage of the overall MNC worldwide (Dunning 1988). For instance, this is the case of core advantages that accrue to the entire organization and are created jointly and shared by all the subsidiaries, like the brand value of Mc Donald's and Coca Cola. Finally, the corporate effect, as we define it and measure it in this paper, also captures the impact of resources and capabilities developed by any particular subsidiary that later spread to the rest of the organization, such as the contribution of integrated players and world product mandates (Bartlett/Ghoshal 1989, Doz/Santos/Williamson 2001).

Corporate Office Impact on MNC Subsidiaries

From the three elements that constitute the corporate effect, we would like to focus particularly on the influence on subsidiaries initiated at the corporate office, along with the theme of this special issue. The role of the corporate office of diversified corporations has been studied by Goold, Campbell, and Alexander (1994). Their analysis of "parenting advantage" can be useful to understand how the MNC headquarters create (or destroy) value for its international subsidiaries, which can be done in four different ways:

1) Stand alone influence: Headquarters' direct impact on the strategy and the organization of each regional unit. Even in highly decentralized MNC, headquarters are typically involved in approving major capital expenditures, in agreeing and monitoring performance targets, and in selecting and motivating the regional units' chief executives. Through this type of decisions that directly affect each subsidiary individually, the headquarters will have an impact on their performance, whose overall average influence in the subsidiaries performance will be captured by the corporate effect.
2) Linkage influence: This type of corporate influence includes all MNC headquarters attempts to promote cooperation and establish inter-unit linkages between the different subsidiaries. How well the MNC headquarters manage these linkages, including for instance transfer of knowledge internally, rotation of managers, and inter-unit coordination mechanisms in general, will also be captured within the overall corporate effect.
3) Central functions and services: Headquarters may centralize certain function and services for the overall MNC. Typically, these are likely to be staff functions, such as finance, central R&D, communications and public relations, and human resources. These activities, often regarded as corporate overhead, also have an impact on the performance of all the subsidiaries within the MNC.
4) Corporate development activities: The decisions about acquisitions, divestments, joint ventures, and alliances are typically carried out by the corporate office. These decisions, in particular the excellence of the corporate office in setting and managing the diversification policy, can also be expected to affect the different subsidiaries and, thus, be included in the overall corporate effect.

Conclusions and Limitations

The results provide clear justification to the study of corporate strategy in multinational corporations. Having detected empirically a MNC corporate effect, future research may investigate why some corporations have a larger impact on their worldwide performance than other MNCs and what the optimal impact may be.

This perspective is very different from earlier analysis in centralization, that concentrated exclusively on the level at which decisions regarding certain activities were made inside MNCs (Gates/Egelhoff 1986) Of course, MNC corporate resources are obviously not all that matters. Industry and regional unit specific effects also exist and they are much more important, each one accounting for 18% and 41% respectively of the variability in performance of MNC across geographical areas. Based on the observed results, we could claim that how well a MNC is managed in different regions and the specific characteristics of the industry in which it is operating have a greater impact in the ultimate profitability of the MNC subsidiaries than the unique characteristics and resources of their parent corporation. In other words, local factors seem to matter more than MNC-level factors. However, they are not the only important sources of performance and MNC-level also contribute to lower-level unit performance.

The results also indicate that the extent of internationalization determines the size of the corporate effect. The evidence of a larger corporate effect for more highly internationalized MNCs contrasts with Roquebert et al. (1996) empirical finding that firms with greater product diversification showed a smaller corporate effect. The results in our paper are consistent with the empirical research that studies the different nature of product and international diversification and their unlike influences on MNC performance (Grant/Jammine/Thomas 1988). We would like to emphasize that, whereas greater product diversification apparently dilutes the effect that corporate resources may have on their businesses, greater internationalization probably allows the MNCs to develop and to leverage to a greater extent their own corporate resources worldwide.

Future research could also analyze the relatively small size of the geographical area effect. The trend toward greater globalization of markets and strategies may be facilitating the internal convergence of the performance of the MNC in different parts of the world, regardless of the unique effect of the regions in which the MNC has activities.

These results, however, should be taken with some caution given particularly the limitations of the dataset. First, the sample is comprised of 76 of the largest American corporations, such as IBM and General Motors. On the one hand, it is not clear to what extent the results can be generalized to smaller firms with international operations, which may differ substantially from established MNCs (Lu/Beamish 2001, McDougall/Oviatt 2000), or to those from a non-USA country of origin, which frequently have very large levels of internationalization. Only replication of this type of study with data from MNCs from other countries and size would shed more light on this issue. Second, given the current impossibility of obtaining comparable performance data at the country level, we had to aggregate the results provided by the Compustat database to four regions in the world in order to have a reasonably balanced design to estimate the different effects. In the search for improved balance, the data obviously lose precision and we will have to wait until new databases become available with sufficiently detailed comparable data to make the entire analysis at the country level. In any case, it is reasonable to believe that the aggregation of data at the regional level may have reduced the estimate for the area effect, but it probably does not have too large an impact on the corporate effect. Third, we have examined the main sources of variance without using control variables that may drive the performance of regional subsidiaries, like extent of diversification. As future studies include different control variables, the corporate effect may be estimated with more precision after discarding other more specific influences on performance. In our opinion, would have we included, for instance, the extent of diversification of the MNCs, the estimate of the corporate effect would have been slightly smaller, since diversification is a decision about corporate development usually taken at the MNC headquarters and, thus, presumably included within our current estimate of the corporate effect. Finally, it should be noted that the estimation of the different effects is based on dummy variables, as it is traditional in the study of source of performance in the strategy field (Rumelt 1991, McGahan/Porter 1997). In this paper, there was no attempt to measure specific types of corporate influence, like the four types of influence discussed above, for instance. The goal was to measure how much of the variability in ROA of MNCs in different geographical areas of the world can be attributed to the MNC as a whole. This is what dummy variables for the MNC (and the other sources of performance variability) allow us to measure, but it does not get into the nature of such effects.

Despite these limitations, the results seem to provide sufficient empirical evidence about the existence of a MNC corporate effect moderated by the extent of internationalization of the MNCs. We hope that more accurate estimates and in different contexts will appear in the international business literature in the future.

Endnotes

1 We would like to thank Anil Gupta, Judy Olian, Stefan Wally, and Gabriel Benito for their helpful comments on an earlier version of this paper
2 For further discussion of this methodology, see Rumelt (1991). Its limitations and one alternative estimation method are discussed in Brush/Bromiley (1997) and Brush/Bromiley/Hendrickx (1999), which obtains substantially larger corporate effects.
3 However, in none of the methods we take into account the possible autocorrelation between observations from different years that belong to the same regional unit. This effect can potentially underestimate the variance of our estimates and therefore inflate artificially the significance of our findings. We test the robustness of our results to the existence of serial autocorrelation by replicating the analysis using just a cross-section of the data with the average ROA for each re-

gional unit. Note that proceeding in this way we could only estimate the effect of three sources of variation: area, industry and corporation, but not the effect of the regional unit, since we cannot be separated from the error term, as Rumelt (1991) explains in detail. Thus, we use only this cross-sectional analysis to check the results. Another possible methodology is Repeated Measures ANOVA. We did not use this methodology because we are intrinsically interested in the interactions with time of the different effects, which constitutes the focus on this alternative method.

4 The cross-sectional analysis based on the average ROA for each regional unit also showed a linear increase in the corporate effect through the three sub-samples.

References

Bartlett, C. A./Ghoshal, S., *Managing Across Borders: The Transnational Solution*, Boston, MA: Harvard Business School Press 1989.
Bowman, E. H./Helfat, C. E., Does Corporate Strategy Matter?, *Strategic Management Journal*, 22, 2001, pp. 1–23.
Brush, T. H./Bromiley, P., What Does a Small Corporate Effect Mean? A Variance Components Simulation of Corporate and Business Effects, *Strategic Management Journal*, 18, 1997, pp. 825–835.
Brush, T. H./Bromiley, P./Hendrickx, M., The Relative Influence of Industry and Corporation on Business Segment Performance: An Alternative Estimate, *Strategic Management Journal*, 20, 1999, pp. 519–548.
Buhner, R., Assessing International Diversification of West German Corporations, *Strategic Management Journal*, 8, 1987, pp. 25–37.
Chandler, A. D., The Functions of the HQ Unit in the Multibusiness Firm, *Strategic Management Journal*, 12, 1991, pp. 31–50.
Delios, A./Beamish, P. W., Geographic Scope, Product Diversification and the Corporate Performance of Japanese Firms, *Strategic Management Journal*, 20, 1999, pp. 711–728.
Dess, G. G./Gupta, A./Hennart, J. F./Hill, C. W. L., Conducting and Integrating Strategy Research at the International, Corporate, and Business Levels: Issues and Directions, *Journal of Management*, 21, 1995, pp. 357–393.
Doz, Y. L./Prahalad, C. K., Headquarters Influence and Strategic Control in MNCs, *Sloan Management Review*, Fall 1981, pp. 15–29.
Doz, Y./Santos, J./Williamson, P., *From Global to Metanational*, Boston, MA: Harvrad Business School Press 2001.
Dunning, J. H., The Eclectic Paradigm of International Production: A Restatement and Some Possible Extensions, *Journal of International Business Studies*, Spring 1988, pp. 1–32.
Ferlie, E./Pettigrew, A., The Nature and Transformation of Corporate Headquarters: A Review of Recent Literature and a Research Agenda, *Journal of Management Studies*, 33, 1996, pp. 495–523.
Gates, S. R./Egelhoff, W. G., Centralization in Headquarters-subsidiary Relationships, *Journal of International Business Studies*, Summer 1986, pp. 71–92.
Geringer, J. M./Beamish, P. W./daCosta, R. C., Diversification Strategy and Internationalization: Implications for MNE Performance, *Strategic Management Journal*, 10, 1989, pp. 109–119.
Goold, M./Campbell, A./Alexander, M., *Corporate-level Strategy*, New York: John Wiley and Sons 1994.
Grant, R. M./Jammine, A. P./Thomas, H., Diversity, Diversification, and Profitability among British Manufacturing Companies, 1972–84, *Academy of Management Journal*, 31, 1988, pp.771–801.
Hansen, G. S./Wernerfelt, B., Determinants of Firm Performance: The Relative Importance of Economic and Organizational factors, *Strategic Management Journal*, 10, 1989, pp. 399–411.

Hill, C. W./Hoskisson, M. E., Strategy and Structure in the Multiproduct Firm, *Academy of Management Review*, 12, 1987, pp. 331–341.
Hitt, M. A./Cheng, J. L. C. (editors), *Managing Trasnational Firms*, Advances in International Management, 14, Amsterdam: JAI Press 2002.
Hitt, M. A./Hoskisson, R. E./Kim, H., International Diversification: Effects on Innovation and Firm Performance in Product-diversified Firms, *Academy of Management Journal*, 40, 1997, pp. 767–798.
Hymer, S., *The International Operations of International Firms: A Study of Direct Investment*, Ph.D. dissertation, MIT 1960.
Kim, W. C./Hwang, P./Burgers, W. P., Global Diversification and Corporate Profit Performance, *Strategic Management Journal*, 10, 1989, pp. 45–57.
Kobrin, S. J., An Empirical Analysis of the Determinants of Global Integration, *Strategic Management Journal*, 12, 1991, pp. 17–31.
Kogut, B., Designing Global Strategies: Profiting from Operational Flexibility, *Sloan Management Review*, 27, 1985, pp. 27–38.
Kogut, B., Normative Observations on the Value Added Chain and Strategic Groups, *Journal of International Business Studies*, 15, 1984, pp. 151–168.
Kogut, B./Zander, U., Knowledge of the Firm and the Evolutionary Theory of the Multinational Corporation, *Journal of International Business Studies*, 4th Quarter 1993, pp. 625–645.
Lu, J. W./Beamish, P. W., The Internationalization and Performance of SMEs, *Strategic Management Journal*, 2, 2001, pp. 565–586.
Martinez, J. I./Jarillo, J. C., The Evolution of Research on Coordination Mechanisms in Multinational Corporations, *Journal of International Business Studies*, Fall 1989, pp. 489–514.
McDougall, P. P./Oviatt, B. M., International Entrepreneurship: The Intersection of Two Research Paths, *Academy of Management Journal*, 43, 2000, pp. 902–908.
McGahan, A. M./Porter, M. E., How Much Industry Matter, Really?, *Strategic Management Journal*, 18, Special Issue, Summer 1997, pp. 15–30.
Nohria, N./Ghoshal, S., Differentiated Fit and Shared Values: Alternatives for Managing Headquarters-subsidiary Relationships, *Strategic Management Journal*, 15, 1994, pp. 491–502.
Porter, M. E., Changing Patterns of International Competition, *California Management Review*, Winter 1986, pp. 9–40.
Powell, T. C., How Much Does Industry Matter? An Alternative Empirical Test, *Strategic Management Journal*, 17, 1996, pp. 232–334.
Roquebert, J. A./Phillips, R. L./Westfall, P. A., Markets vs. Management: What 'Drives' Profitability?, *Strategic Management Journal*, 17, 1996, pp. 653–664.
Roth, K./Schweiger, D. M./Morrison, A. J., Global Strategy Implementation at the Business Unit Level: Operational Capabilities and Administrative Mechanisms, *Journal of International Business Studies*, 3rd Quarter 1991, pp. 369–402.
Rugman, A. M., *International Diversification and the Multinational Enterprise*, Lexington, MA: Lexington Books 1979.
Rugman, A. M., *Inside the Multinationals: The Economics of International Markets*, Lexington, MA: Lexington books 1981.
Rumelt, R. P., How Much Does Industry Matter?, *Strategic Management Journal*, 12, 1991, pp. 167–185.
Schmalensee, R., Do Markets Differ Much?, *American Economic Review*, 75, 1985, pp. 341–351.

mir *Edition*

Tobias Specker

Postmerger – Management in den ost- und mitteleuropäischen Transformationsstaaten

2002, XX, 431 pages, Br., € 64,– (approx. US $ 58.–)
ISBN 3-409-12010-6

Since the beginning of the transformation process in the Middle and Eastern European countries, German companies have put a special emphasis on entering these markets via corporate acquisitions. Tobias Specker analyses the critical issue of postmerger management with a specific focus on the particular transformation context. His theoretical reflections are supported by results of an explorative study of various German companies.

The book is addressed to lecturers and students of international management. Consultants and managers will also receive valuable information.

Betriebswirtschaftlicher Verlag Dr. Th. Gabler GmbH, Abraham-Lincoln-Str. 46, 65189 Wiesbaden

Alfredo J. Mauri/Rakesh B. Sambharya

The Performance Implications of a Global Integration Strategy in Global Industries: An Empirical Investigation Using Inter-area Product Flows[1]

Abstract

- Several authors in international management have stressed the importance of global integration for firms competing internationally. Surprisingly, little empirical research has been conducted on the relationship between global integration and performance.

- This paper suggests that the performance consequences of global integration require balancing the configuration benefits and the coordination requirements of a global strategy. This leads to a non-linear relation between global integration and firm performance.

Key Results

- This study provides evidence of this non-linear relationship by operationalizing global integration as inter-area product flows on a sample of US firms competing in global industries. These results highlight the benefits of global integration in developing competitive advantage, but also indicate the difficulties of configuring and coordinating interdependent activities internationally.

Authors

Alfredo J. Mauri, Assistant Professor of Management and Information Systems, Department of Management, Saint Joseph's University, Philadelphia, PA, USA.

Rakesh B. Sambharya, Associate Professor of Management, School of Business, Rutgers University – Camden, Camden, NJ, USA.

Introduction

Several international management scholars have focused on the role of global integration of activities for firms pursuing a global strategy (Bartlett/Ghoshal 1987, Hout/Porter/Rudden 1982, Roth 1995). The global integration of a company's operations is a response to the fundamental nature of global competition (Ghemawat/Spence 1986) and represents a key dimension of an international strategy (Kutschker/Baurle 1997, Prahalad/Doz 1987). Global integration indicates the importance given by the international firm to geographically disperse and specialize its operations with the intention of building sources of competitive advantage (Porter 1986).

Global competition is becoming commonplace in many industries. Host countries have liberalized regulations concerning the foreign control of assets and have reduced tariff barriers. By allowing the free movement of goods across borders, trade liberalization promotes the establishment of global integration strategies. Multinational enterprises (MNEs) are globalizing at a frantic pace to meet this increasingly global competition and achieve economies of scope and scale. MNEs are relocating operations globally in an unending search for cost efficiencies and location economies.

However, despite the theoretical and practical importance of global integration, surprisingly little empirical research has been done on this topic. This study investigates the performance implications of a strategy of global integration by constructing an index of global integration based on inter-area product flows (Kobrin 1991, Mauri/Phatak 2001). Using a sample of US MNEs in four global industries for the period 1992–1997, empirical results show evidence of a curvilinear relationship between global integration and performance. For low and high levels of global integration, the global integration index is related negatively to MNE performance; however, at moderate levels of global integration a positive relation with performance is found.

Theoretical Framework

The MNE Network and Global Integration

Current theoretical developments in organizational theory consider the MNE as an interorganizational network (Andersson/Forsgren 2000, Ghoshal/Bartlett 1990, Ghoshal/Nohria 1989, Malnight 1996). The network view suggests that an MNE is a collection of differentiated units, operating in different parts of the world, and using various organizational modes (Ghoshal/Nohria 1989). The genesis of the network view lies in the seminal works by Emerson (1962), Pfeffer and Salancik (1978) and Thompson (1967), who examine various organizational issues based on an analysis of critical resources and resource linkages among network members. Their research explores power-dependency relations (Emerson 1962), a firm's adaptation and survival based on the access to scarce resources held by a limited number of external actors (Pfeffer/Salancik 1978), and the notion of resource interdependencies influencing the fit between an organization's administrative structure and the environment (Thompson 1967).

A highly interdependent network implies significant and frequent resource linkages and exchange across units. In an MNE, this resource exchange occurs between the parent company and the highly specialized subsidiaries, and among the subsidiaries themselves. As a result of the increasing network differentiation and integration needed to effectively compete internationally, the subsidiaries become interdependent nodes, and their outputs become inputs to other units located in other countries.

Consistent with the network view, a growing research stream in international management has attributed a more prominent role to the subsidiary (Andersson/Forsgren 2000, Birkinshaw/Hood 1998, Malnight 1996). According to this literature, some foreign subsidiaries become centers of excellence (Andersson/Forsgren 2000) that contribute key resources to the rest of the MNE by making use of subsidiary initiatives (Birkinshaw/Morrison 1995) or global mandates (Roth/Morrison 1992). Thus the subsidiary has a significant role in the MNE network since it possesses its own advantage and may even be an equal partner for headquarters (Andersson/Forsgren 2000, Birkinshaw/Hood 1998).

The integration of global operations can be gauged by the international resource exchange between interdependent MNE units (Bartlett/Ghoshal 1987, Ghoshal 1987, Gupta/Govindarajan 1991, Kobrin 1991). This exchange involves several types of resource flows: product and components, financial capital, and knowledge. Bartlett and Ghoshal (1987) and Kobrin (1991) underscore the importance of the product exchange compared to other resource flows. Bartlett and Ghoshal (1987, p. 48) suggest that product interdependence is the "most fundamental" among the resource exchanges. Product flows in globally integrated companies exhibit high frequency and lead to critical operational interdependencies requiring complex coordination processes.

Intra-firm trade statistics reveal the magnitude of the international product flows between units of MNE networks. Approximately 20 years ago, intrafirm shipments accounted for 24 percent of the entire US manufacturing trade (Hipple 1990). This fraction has become even more pronounced in recent years. The aggregate value of intrafirm exports has fluctuated between 32 and 40 percent of US exports in goods, and between 37 and 43 percent of US imports in goods, for the period 1982–1994 (Zeile 1997). The most recent statistics available from the

US Bureau of Economic Analysis (Mataloni Jr/Yorgason 2002, Zeile 2001) show that intrafirm trade is currently at a level of 34 percent of US exports and 38 percent of US imports. This increase in magnitude over previous years indicates the importance accorded to global integration by US MNEs.

According to the network view, the globally integrating MNE faces two fundamental challenges: the geographic configuration of value-adding activities, and the coordination of those activities (Porter 1986). The configuration dimension involves arranging the overall system of MNE activities, including selecting the geographic location and defining the scope of responsibilities of each MNE unit; while coordination implies building the administrative mechanisms that enable the MNE to effectively organize its geographically dispersed units.

The Configuration of the Integrated Network in a Global Industry

Market structure and firm-specific factors affect the configuration of the integrated network for an MNE competing in a global industry. Market structure represents the technical and economic conditions that provide the context for industry competition, and which influence strategy choices and performance levels for the firms participating in an industry (Bain 1968, Scherer/Ross 1990). Porter (1986) suggests that global industries present converging patterns of competition "where a firm must in some way integrate its activities on a worldwide basis to capture the linkages among countries" (p. 19).

More specifically on the geographic configuration of global industries, Porter (1986) proposes that global competition is shaped by substantial upfront investments for creating new technologies and scale economies, as well as by the establishment of specialized subsidiaries in countries that offer the most attractive conditions. Another aspect of configuration lies in standardizing products and components to achieve cost reduction due to the convergence of consumer needs (Levitt 1983). Furthermore, Ohmae (1990) suggests that the expectations for building a global base provide strong incentives for an MNE to make large and specialized investments before it can take the products to their respective markets and generate revenues.

In contrast to the market structure explanations, firm-specific forces illustrate the influence of a firm's unique resources on the integration configuration of the MNE. Internalization theory (Dunning 1988) and transaction costs theory (Caves 1996, Hennart 1991, Teece 1986) suggest that firm-specific resources and location factors encourage the global firm to internalize value-adding activities abroad. The firm-specific resources provide an ownership advantage that enable the globally integrated company to develop and transfer knowledge and other resources internationally in a more efficient manner than if it used market transactions; while location factors influence where these value-adding activities are internalized.

Similarly, the resource-based view examines a firm's collection of specific resources to explain the sustainability of its competitive advantage. (Barney 1991, Conner 1991, Wernerfelt 1984). This resource advantage is difficult to imitate because of the long time periods required in developing firm-specific resource stocks (Dierickx/Cool 1989); the irreversible nature of the investments (Ghemawat 1991); and the uncertainty, complexity, and conflict that occurs while developing resources (Amit/Schoemaker 1993). The resource-based perspective suggests that the essence of a firm's competitive advantage resides in its ability to create, transfer and combine new knowledge efficiently across organizational units. Several authors have clearly illustrated the constant search for knowledge and technological developments in global industries (Ghoshal 1987, Ghoshal/Bartlett 1988, Kobrin 1991, Mauri/Phatak 2001, Roth/Morrison 1990). Consistent with this view, Kogut and Zander (1992) suggest that new knowledge and learning result from a firm's "combinative abilities" to generate new applications from existing knowledge and that these abilities are embedded in the social relations across members of the network.

In summary, configuring an integrated network requires arranging activities consistent with the characteristics of global industries, as well as with the internalization of firm-specific resources. While the industry forces call for convergent competitive patterns, firm-specific forces lead to the creation of competitive advantage.

Coordination of the Network

The information-processing theory of the MNE (Egelhoff 1982, Egelhoff 1991, Sambharya/Phatak 1990) provides a useful framework to examine the coordination demands of the dispersed and interdependent activities of the global MNE. Information-processing theory focuses on organizational adaptation to uncertainty. Galbraith (1973) defines uncertainty as "... the difference between the amount of information required to perform the task and the amount of information already possessed by the organization" (p. 5). The essence of information-processing theory is that the information-processing requirements due to uncertainty in the environment should be matched with the information-processing capacities created by the organization (Galbraith 1973, Tushman/Nadler 1978).

With respect to global integration, the coordination of interdependent activities is difficult because the global company operates in several countries in environments characterized by a high degree of rivalry. According to the information-processing theory (Egelhoff 1991, Tushman/Nadler 1978), globally interdependent activities call for the creation of coordination mechanisms able to handle the complexity inherent to a global strategy.

Several studies illustrate the increasing requirements for information processing associated with international integration. Empirical studies of MNE operations indicate the important of balancing information processing requirements with information processing capacities in the form of establishing the appropriate organizational structure (Habib/Victor 1991, Stopford/Wells 1972). The headquarter-subsidiary literature (Ghoshal/Nohria 1989, Gupta/Govindarajan 1991, Martinez/Jarillo 1991) illustrates the process of establishing the requisite coordination capacity by adjusting other dimensions of organizational structure such as centralization, formalization, integrative mechanisms and socialization. Furthermore, other studies suggest that information-processing capacity can be increased by the simultaneous use of formal and informal control mechanisms, such as the creation of shared values (Baliga/Jaeger 1984), the use of information and career planning systems (Prahalad/Doz 1987), and the improvement of inter-unit communication patterns (Ghoshal/Korine/Szulanski 1994).

Hypotheses on the Influence of Global Integration on MNE Performance

This paper is based on the premise that the performance consequences of a global integration strategy can be examined by looking at the net balance between benefits and costs of global integration and coordination. We propose that for firms competing in global industries the performance implications of a global integration strategy differ for low, moderate, and high levels of global integration. As a result of these differences, the relation between global integration and performance follows a non-linear pattern.

Consistent with the previous discussion, firms with low levels of global integration have strong incentives to configure an integrated network by conforming to the market structure forces of global competition and by building firm-specific resources. This network configuration has the potential to increase profitability because of scale economies and learning, and because the investments in firm-specific resources can be leveraged across international markets. However, building a collection of firm-specific resources requires substantial investments and takes considerable time. While building these resources, the incremental costs are likely to outweigh the benefits because of the difficulties in the accumulation process when building firm-specific resources. In addition, inter-temporal tradeoffs between the long-term benefits and current costs (Laverty 1996) for developing and deploying this ownership advantage contribute to a negative balance affecting firm performance in the short-term.

Several empirical studies have documented the strong links between investments in firm-specific resources in the form of intangible assets, and the international expansion of firms. Regarding global integration, studies by Kobrin (1991) and Mauri and Phatak (2001) showed evidence of the positive link between the development of intangibles assets, such as those produced by R & D and advertising, and the deployment of a global integration strategy. Similarly, Kotabe and colleagues (2002) and Morck and Yeung (1991) studied the moderating role of intangible assets in increasing the profitability of an MNE's international expansion. These studies suggest that investments in ownership advantage support the internationalization of firms. However, notwithstanding the long-term value of intangible assets, accounting rules treat the development of intangibles as current expenses with an immediate negative impact on firm profitability. This is particularly important for firms with low levels of global integration since as a consequence of the temporal tradeoff, the investments supporting the configuration of a globally integrated network may take years to become profitable.

According to information-processing theory, a firm's performance depends on its ability to build the appropriate organizational structures and effective coordination mechanisms to match the requirements for information processing. Firms may experience temporal setbacks during the initial phases of the global integration process. Kogut and Zander (1992, 1993) highlight the difficulties for creating an appropriate collaborative context for transferring tacit knowledge across MNE units. They argue that it takes considerable time and investments to build the combinative abilities between units of an MNE network to create and transfer new knowledge effectively. These delays may contribute to a negative balance between benefits and costs for firms willing to increase their commitment to become more global.

Consequently, for low levels of global integration the difficulties of developing the firm-specific resources required in a network configuration and the intertemporal tradeoffs when building such resources, as well as possible delays in building a collaborative network context are likely to result in a negative balance between benefits and costs. Hence, the following hypothesis is proposed:

Hypothesis 1 (H1). At low levels of global integration, global integration is negatively related to firm performance.

In contrast, at moderate levels of global integration, the benefits of an integrated network allow global firms to increase performance in relation to their rivals by the use of national differences, economies of scale and scope, and global learning and innovation (Ghoshal 1987, Porter 1986). Under these conditions, an MNE is likely to realize the benefits of the investments in firm-specific resources and reap the rewards of configuring an integrated network of geographically dispersed units. Regarding coordination, at moderate levels of global integration we expect that on average MNEs will be able to perform well given the moderate information-processing requirements and the availability of the several coordinating mechanisms outlined above. Furthermore, the larger exposure and longer experience at integrating the operations of interdependent units create a collaborative context encouraging innovations and entrepreneurial actions from employees operating within the network of subsidiaries. Therefore:

Hypothesis 2 (H2). At moderate levels of global integration, global integration is positively related to firm performance.

As global integration becomes high, the costs of managing and operating an integrated network of subsidiaries may begin to outweigh the benefits. Specifically, high levels of reciprocal interdependence (Thompson 1967) across the network produce strong demands for tightly coordinating activities and leave firms with a small margin of error. Under these demanding conditions it is likely that coordinating mechanisms may fail, and the firm's information-processing capacities are not up to the requirements of high global integration levels. In this case, the structural mechanisms are likely to be overwhelmed and lead to bottlenecks and breakdowns. This in turn will lead to delays and administrative problems that could disrupt operations and flows of information. Ultimately, any prolonged disruption could affect the firm's financial performance.

Levy (1995) developed a conceptual framework in which distance can reduce the advantages derived from the national differences owing to increases in inventory, high lead time, unfulfilled demand, and high transportation costs. Using a case study of a personal computer company and a subsequent simulation, Levy shows that these factors may have a significant effect on the costs of sourcing parts and components internationally. Consequently, the complex interdependencies are likely to lead to lower performance levels because the firm is likely to experience coordination problems.

As a result, a firm can handle global integration only up to a certain point; past that point, breakdowns occur due to overload in the system. The MNE is unlikely to succeed at building the appropriate information-processing capacities to match the overwhelming information-processing requirements at high levels of global integration. Consequently, we propose the following hypothesis:

Hypothesis 3 (H3). At high levels of global integration, global integration is negatively related to firm performance.

Methodology

Sample Selection

The sample of companies used to test the previous hypotheses was created from industries in which global integration may be assumed relevant for developing a competitive advantage. We selected the top four industries based on the Index of Transnational Integration reported by Kobrin (1991, p. 22). These include the computer equipment (SIC 357), communications equipment (SIC 366), electronic components (SIC 367) and motor vehicles (SIC 371) industries. Previous studies have also considered these industries to be of a global nature (Bartlett 1986, Birkinshaw/Morrison/Hulland 1995, Flaherthy 1986, Hout/Porter/Rudden 1982, Johansson/Yip 1994, Levy 1995, Porter 1986, Roth/Morrison 1990, Takeuchi/Porter 1986). Companies were included in the sample according to their participation in the selected industries, as indicated by the primary SIC code from COMPUSTAT. Only firms with annual revenues greater than $50 million were selected. In addition, the level of international exposure was controlled by only including companies that derive a minimum of 10 percent of sales from overseas operations (Daniels/Pitts/Tretter 1985, Habib/Victor 1991, Palepu 1985) and that explicitly disclose inter-area sales in their financial statements. Thus the sample resulted in 69 firms with a complete data series during the period 1992 to 1997 for a total of 414 firm-year observations.

Measurement of Independent and Dependent Variables

Global Integration Index

The index of global integration was based on intrafirm trade among corporate units in different geographic areas. Studies by Kobrin (1991) and Mauri and Phatak (2001) consider the inter-subsidiary product flows as an indicator of global integration. More specifically, the index of global integration was operationalized as follows:

$$GI_t = \sum_j IS_{jt} / (\text{Total company sales})_t,$$

– in which IS_{jt} refers to the inter-area sales reported in year t from subsidiaries located in area j to other geographic regions where the firm has operations. This index reflects the percentage of total sales that is within the firm and across geographic regions as an indicator for global integration of a company in year t. This information was collected from the financial statements of US companies.

According to the Financial Accounting Standards No. 14 (FAS 14), companies are required to disclose information on their operations in geographic areas that represent sales or assets greater than 10 percent of the amounts presented in the consolidated financial statements. In addition to inter-area sales, sales to unaffiliated customers, identifiable assets, and operating income are disclosed. This information is usually included as a note to the financial statements.

The global integration index was created from sales of units directly or indirectly controlled by the parent company (the accounting criterion for consolidating sales of affiliated units is direct and indirect ownership by the parent company of more than 50 percent). Hence, sales from joint ventures or affiliates in which the parent company owns less than or equal to 50 percent are excluded from the index.

Control Variables

Several control variables that may have an impact on performance were included as controls: firm size, leverage, product diversification, level of internationalization, and industry effects. The data source for constructing all control variables was COMPUSTAT. Firm size was constructed to control for possible economies of scale at the corporate level, and was measured by calculating the log of sales for each year in the period 1992–1997. Leverage has been argued to be associated with financial performance (Jensen 1989) and has been used in previous studies examining the relation between internationalization and firm performance (Hitt/Hoskisson/Kim 1997, Tallman/Li 1996). Leverage was constructed using the fraction of total debt to total assets by firm and year. Similarly, product diversification was operationalized using an entropy index of diversification (Palepu 1985) from four-digit SIC segments sales. This index was calculated as:

$$ST_t = \sum_k S_{kt} \ln(1/S_{kt}),$$

– in which S_{kt} is the share of total company sales of each four-digit SIC industry segment k during year t. The diversification index was calculated for each year in the period 1992–1997. The level of internationalization was measured using the ratio of international assets to total assets for each year in the period 1992–1997. Industry effects were added as a control variable in the regression model using dummies for the industry groups.

Firm Performance

The dependent variable was measured using Return on Sales (ROS) for each year in the period 1992 to 1997 from COMPUSTAT. Return on sales was calculated as net income before extraordinary items divided by sales. The sales denominator reduces potential distortions while measuring firm performance because sales are generally expressed in more current monetary terms than total assets (Geringer/Beamish/daCosta 1989).

Statistical Methodology

We used the Prais-Winsten regression that corrects for serial correlations. The Prais-Winsten method uses a generalized least-squares estimator. The most common autocorrelated error process is the first-order auto-regressive process. Under this assumption, the linear regression can be written as $Y_t = \beta X_t + u_t$, where the errors satisfy $u_t = \varrho u_{t-1} + e_t$, and e_t is independent and identically distributed as $N(0, \sigma^2)$. The Prais-Winsten method provides a transformed Durbin-Watson statistic, useful in evaluating the removal of autocorrelation.

In the first model, we ran the regression using all control variables and the linear term of the global integration index. We then sequentially added the quadratic term of the global integration index in the second model. Finally we added the cubic term of global integration index in the third model. This methodology enables testing the proposed set of hypotheses. In particular, we expect negative regression coefficients for the linear and cubic terms of the global integration index, while the quadratic term should yield a positive coefficient.

Because of possible multicolinearity between the linear, quadratic and cubic terms of the global integration index, we followed the methodology developed by Jaccard, Turrisi, and Wan (1990). This procedure uses a "mean-centering" approach, originally proposed by Cronbach (1987), in which the linear variable is mean-centered before constructing its respective quadratic and cubic terms. This procedure also requires testing whether adding the quadratic and cubic terms to the regression equation indeed increase the explanatory power of the base model using the linear global integration term, the control variables and the auto-regressive factor.

Results

Table 1 shows descriptive statistics of the variables used in the sample.

Table 2 shows the results of the Prais-Winsten regression models using return on sales (ROS) as the dependent variable. For the firms sampled, the regression coefficients for the "mean-centered" linear, quadratic and cubic terms of global integration were similar to those obtained using the original global integration

Table 1. Descriptive Statistics

Variable	Mean	S.D.	1	2	3	4	5
1. Size (log sales)	7.22	1.78					
2. Leverage	0.42	0.18	−0.01				
3. Product diversification	0.24	0.36	0.18***	0.02			
4. International assets	0.24	0.16	0.46***	0.18***	−0.23***		
5. Global integration index	0.16	0.22	0.22***	−0.05	−0.31***	0.43***	
6. Return on sales	0.05	0.08	0.09$^\psi$	−0.45***	−0.02	−0.05	0.05

N = 414
ψ p < 0.1, *** p < 0.001

variable. In order to facilitate the interpretation of the global integration regression coefficients, the results shown in Table 2 correspond to the original global integration index without the transformation.

As can be seen in Table 2, the regression results for Models 1 to 3 explain a considerable portion of the variation of performance for the companies sampled. The total R-squares, including both the regression model and first order auto-regressive error, range from 37.6 to almost 40 percent of the variation of firm performance. Of this total, the regression component explains between 13 to 16 percent of this variation, while the auto-regressive component represents the remaining 23 to 24 percent. The strong statistical significance of the auto-regressive coefficients across Models 1 to 3 confirms the relevance of this auto-regressive source. In addition, the Durbin-Watson coefficient in the three models showed a value close to 2, indicating the removal of the first-order serial autocorrelation.

Regarding the control variables, firm size was positively related to ROS, but only significant at the 0.10 level in model 2, and at the 0.05 level in Model 3. The leverage regression coefficient showed a negative and strongly significant association between leverage and performance for all regression models. This relation is consistent with previous studies (Hitt/Hoskisson/Kim 1997, Tallman/Li 1996) and indicates a tendency for highly leveraged firms to present lower performance levels. Neither product diversification nor international assets were significantly related to ROS.

Regarding global integration, the regression results show evidence supporting a non-linear relation between the index of global integration and firm performance. As can be seen in Model 1, the combination of the linear term of the global integration index, the control variables and the auto-regressive component are able to explain to 37.6 percent of the total variation of ROS. By adding the quadratic term of the global integration index to the regression equation in Model 2, the total R-square increases by 0.6 percentage points over the R-square of Model 1. This

Table 2. Results of Prais-Winsten Regression

Independent variables	Dependent variable: ROS		
	Model 1	Model 2	Model 3
Firm size (log sales)	0.005	0.006^ψ	0.007*
	(1.56)	(1.92)	(2.17)
Leverage	−0.156***	−0.160***	−0.164***
	(−6.62)	(−6.83)	(−7.04)
Product diversification	0.007	0.004	0.000
	(0.44)	(0.25)	(0.00)
International assets	−0.015	−0.003	0.010
	(−0.42)	(−0.09)	(0.28)
Computer industry dummy	0.013	0.019	0.027^ψ
	(0.97)	(1.40)	(1.94)
Communications industry dummy	−0.017	−0.007	0.003
	(−1.00)	(−0.38)	(0.17)
Electronic components industry dummy	0.028	0.033*	0.034*
	(1.91)	(2.25)	(2.35)
Global integration index	−0.0002	−0.090^ψ	−0.330***
	(−0.01)	(−1.80)	(−3.53)
Global integration index square		0.088*	0.706***
		2.05	(3.38)
Global integration index cube			−0.336**
			(−3.02)
Constant	0.068**	0.063*	0.063*
	(2.72)	(2.52)	(2.55)
Auto-regressive coefficient	−0.419***	−0.412***	−0.412***
	(−9.27)	(−9.08)	(−9.07)
Regression R-squareⁱ	0.1319***	0.1426***	0.1617***
Total R-square	0.3755***	0.3817***	0.3955***
Change in Total R-square	–	0.0062*	0.0200**
Durbin-Watson	1.9651	1.9574	1.9489

t-statistic in parentheses
ψ $p < 0.1$, * $p < 0.05$, ** $p < 0.01$, *** $p < 0.001$
[i] Includes the regression component of the model, excludes the first order auto-regressive error component.

increment is statistically significant with a p-value of 0.0449 ($F = 4.05$; $df = 1,403$).

In Model 3, adding the quadratic and cubic terms of the global integration index, simultaneously, showed a much stronger increase in R-square. In Model 3, the total R-square increases 2 percentage points over Model 1. This change in total R-square is statistically significant with a p-value of 0.0015 ($F = 6.63$; $df = 2,402$). Furthermore, the comparison of Model 2 and Model 3 shows the individual contribution of the cubic term of global integration to the explanatory power of the regression model. In this case, R-square changes from 38.2 percent in model 2 to 39.6 percent in model 3. This increase of 1.4 percentage points has a p-value of 0.0027 (F = 9.14 df = 1,402), hence confirming the significant contribution of the cubic term.

Finally, in Model 3, the sign of the regression coefficients for the linear, quadratic and cubic terms of the global integration index are consistent with the proposed hypotheses. Both coefficients for the linear and cubic terms showed a significant negative association with firm performance. In contrast, the coefficient of the quadratic term of the global integration index was positive and highly significant. The signs of these coefficients provide evidence supporting the hypotheses that low and high levels of global integration are negatively associated with firm performance (*H1* and *H3*), while moderate levels of global integration are positively associated with firm performance *(H2)*.

Figure 1 shows a graphical representation of the relation between global integration and firm performance according to the regression results of Model 3. This curve shows how the average level of ROS varies in relation to the global integration index in sampled firms.

Figure 1. Graphical Representation of the Relation between the Global Integration Index and ROS*

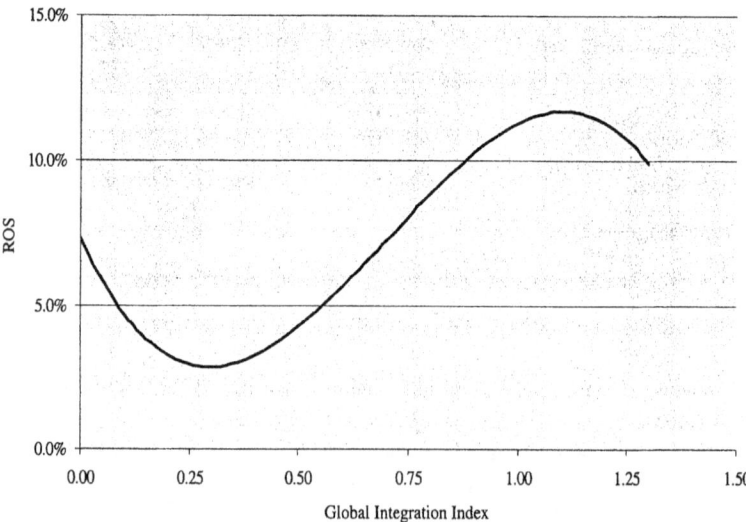

* Calculated from the regression results of Model 3 and using the Global integration index as the independent variable. The computer industry dummy variable was set to 1 and other dummy variables to zero, all other regression variables were held constant using their respective sample means.

Discussion and Conclusions

The Prais-Winsten regression results for Models 2 and 3 suggest the existence of a non-linear relationship between the global integration index and performance. The results of Model 3 show that low and high levels of global integration are associated negatively to firm profitability. In addition, the middle segment has a positive slope as suggested by the significance of the regression coefficient for the quadratic term of the global integration index. These findings support the view that the benefits derived from integrating operations globally (Ghoshal 1987, Porter 1986) may be offset by the costs of managing and coordinating distant international operations between the headquarters and subsidiaries and across subsidiaries themselves (Bartlett 1986, Davidson/Haspeslagh 1982, Levy 1995).

These results are consistent with the network view of the MNE. As can be seen in Figure 1, the left and negative portion of the curve represents the "threshold" to global integration. The negative slope in this section is consistent with the obstacles for developing and deploying the firm-specific resources that support the configuration of the integrated network. This negative segment also illustrates the efforts by the MNE for developing the necessary scale economies consistent with the market structure forces of global industries. The middle segment of the curve represents the "realization" of the global integration potential and suggests that moderate levels of intra-firm product flows result in an effective deployment of a global strategy across interdependent MNE units. This portion of the curve suggests that a global firm can achieve a competitive advantage by creating an integrated network of interdependent units.

Further, the right negative segment of the curve represents the "limits" of global integration. This negative section suggests the managerial boundaries for creating a network of specialized and geographically dispersed units. As illustrated in Figure 1, this negative segment represents a global integration index beyond 100 percent, and implies inter-area segment sales larger than a firm's annual sales to its external customers. At this level, the intra-firm product flows create excessive interdependencies that produce a tremendous strain on the organizational system. This segment highlights the dilemma faced by MNEs from the information-processing perspective. At very high levels of globalization, even mature and experienced MNEs have difficulty coping with the enormous information-processing requirements, and are likely to find their information capacities inadequate.

The managerial implication of integrating international product flows among MNE units is that global integration has costs as well as benefits. Firms are likely to start their internationalization process by exporting or serving local markets through local production. As firms become more internationalized, global integration becomes both feasible and profitable. Global integration allows companies to develop a competitive advantage by use of national differences, and economies of scale and scope. However, the integration of operations also brings coordination costs. The evidence found in this study clearly points in the direction of a non-linear relation between the index of global integration and performance. Managers should be aware of the difficulties of developing and coordinating their interdependent international operations. The negative relation between integration and performance at low levels of global integration implies that managers should realize that the firm needs to be prepared to sustain heavy costs before the benefits of the integration strategy are realized. Furthermore, at moderate levels of integration they should be aware that more integration is not necessarily better, and thus some activities may rather remain "decoupled."

This study has several limitations. One clear limitation refers to the issue of causality between global integration and performance. The Prais-Wisten regression is a cross-sectional methodology that permits correcting for serial autocorrelation. A more rigorous test would require examining how longitudinal changes in the global integration index affect changes in MNE performance. Another limitation is the selection of sampled firms from only four global industries. It may be interesting to evaluate the generalizability of the non-linear results by selecting firms from other industries in which global integration may have competitive relevance. One more limitation refers to the use of only one archival measure of global integration based on inter-area exchange of products. As the use of questionnaires is a common technique to collect data on the topic of global strategy, a methodology combining primary and archival sources can be used to validate the results of this study. This combined methodology may be applied to examine how other dimensions of global integration may affect MNE performance. Future research could continue to measure global integration as the inter-area product exchange disclosed in financial statements and enhance our understanding of the complex relation between global strategy and performance.

Acknowledgement

1 The authors thank Niels Noorderhaven and two anonymous reviewers for their insightful comments on earlier versions of this paper.

References

Amit, R./Schoemaker, P. J. H., Strategic Assets and Organizational Rent, *Strategic Management Journal*, 14, 1, 1993, pp. 33–46.
Andersson, U./Forsgren, M., In Search of Centre of Excellence: Network Embeddedness and Subsidiary Roles in Multinational Corporations, *Management International Review*, 40, 4, 2000, pp. 329–350.
Bain, J. S., *Industrial Organization*, New York, NY: Wiley 1968.
Baliga, B. R./Jaeger, A., Multinational Corporations: Control Systems and Delegation Issues, *Journal of International Business Studies*, 15, 2, 1984, pp. 25–40.
Barney, J., Firm Resources and Sustained Competitive Advantage, *Journal of Management*, 17, 1, 1991, pp. 99–120.
Bartlett, C. A., Building and Managing the Transnational: The New Organizational Challenge, in Porter, M. E. (ed), *Competition in Global Industries*, Boston: Harvard Business School Press 1986, pp. 367–401.
Bartlett, C. A./Ghoshal, S., Managing Across Borders: New Organizational Responses, *Sloan Management Review*, 29, 1, 1987, pp. 43–53.
Birkinshaw, J./Hood, N., Multinational Subsidiary Evolution: Capability and Charter Change in Foreign-Owned Subsidiary Companies, *The Academy of Management Review*, 23, 4, 1998, pp. 773–795.
Birkinshaw, J./Hood, N./Jonsson, S., Building Firm-Specific Advantages in Multinational Corporations: The Role of Subsidiary Initiative, *Strategic Management Journal*, 19, 3, 1998, pp. 221–241.
Birkinshaw, J./Morrison, A./Hulland, J., Structural and Competitive Determinants of a Global Integration Strategy, *Strategic Management Journal*, 16, 8, 1995, pp. 637–655.
Birkinshaw, J. M./Morrison, A. J., Configurations of Strategy and Structure in Subsidiaries of Multinational Corporations, *Journal of International Business Studies*, 26, 4, 1995, pp. 729–753.
Caves, R. E., *Multinational Enterprise and Economic Analysis*, Cambridge, MA: Cambridge University Press 1996.
Conner, K. R., A Historical Comparison of Resource-Based Theory and Five Schools of Thought Within Industrial Organization Economics: Do We Have a Theory of the Firm?, *Journal of Management*, 17, 1, 1991, pp. 121–154.
Cronbach, L. J., Statistical Tests for Moderator Variables: Flaws in Analyses Recently Proposed, *Psychological Bulletin*, 102, 3, 1987, pp. 414–417.
Daniels, J. D./Pitts, R. A./Tretter, M. J., Organizing for Dual Strategies of Product Diversity and International Expansion, *Strategic Management Journal*, 6, 3, 1985, pp. 223–237.
Davidson, W. H./Haspeslagh, P., Shaping a Global Product Organization, *Harvard Business Review*, 60, 4, 1982, pp. 125–132.
Dierickx, I./Cool, K., Asset Stock Accumulation and Sustainability of Competitive Advantage; Comment; Reply, *Management Science*, 35, 12, 1989, pp. 1504–1514.
Dunning, J. H., The Eclectic Paradigm of International Production: A Restatement and Some Possible Extensions, *Journal of International Business Studies*, 19, 1, 1988, pp. 1–31.
Egelhoff, W. G., Strategy and Structure in Multinational Corporations: An Information-Processing Approach, *Administrative Science Quarterly*, 27, 3, 1982, pp. 435–458.
Egelhoff, W. G., Information-Processing Theory and the Multinational Enterprise, *Journal of International Business Studies*, 22, 3, 1991, pp. 341–368.
Emerson, R. M., Power-Dependence Relations, *American Sociological Review*, 27, 1962, pp. 31–41.
Flaherthy, M. T., Coordinating International Manufacturing and Technology, in Porter, M. (ed), *Competition in Global Industries*, Boston: Harvard Business School Press 1986, pp. 83–110.
Galbraith, J. R., *Designing Complex Organizations*, Reading, MA: Adison-Wesley Publishing Company 1973.
Geringer, J. M./Beamish, P. W./daCosta, R. C., Diversification Strategy and Internationalization: Implications for MNE Performance, *Strategic Management Journal*, 10, 2, 1989, pp. 109–119.
Ghemawat, P., *Commitment: The Dynamic of Strategy*, New York, NY: The Free Press 1991.

Ghemawat, P./Spence, A. M., Modeling Global Competition, in Porter, M. (ed), *Competition in Global Industries*, Boston: Harvard Business School Press 1986, pp. 61–79.
Ghoshal, S., Global Strategy: An Organizing Framework, *Strategic Management Journal*, 8, 5, 1987, pp. 425–440.
Ghoshal, S./Bartlett, C. A., Creation, Adoption, and Diffusion of Innovations by Subsidiaries of Multinational Corporations, *Journal of International Business Studies*, 19, 3, 1988, pp. 365–388.
Ghoshal, S./Bartlett, C. A., The Multinational Corporation as an Interorganizational Network, *Academy of Management Review*, 15, 4, 1990, pp. 603–625.
Ghoshal, S./Korine, H./Szulanski, G., Interunit Communication in Multinational Corporations, *Management Science*, 40, 1, 1994, pp. 96–110.
Ghoshal, S./Nohria, N., Internal Differentiation Within Multinational Corporations, *Strategic Management Journal*, 10, 4, 1989, pp. 323–337.
Gupta, A. K./Govindarajan, V., Knowledge Flows and the Structure of Control Within Multinational Corporations, *Academy of Management Review*, 16, 4, 1991, pp. 768–792.
Habib, M. M./Victor, B., Strategy, Structure, and Performance of US Manufacturing and Service MNCs: A Comparative Analysis, *Strategic Management Journal*, 12, 8, 1991, pp. 589–606.
Hennart, J.-F., The Transaction Cost Theory of the Multinational Enterprise, in Pitelis, C. N./Sugden, R. (eds), *The Nature of the Transnational Firm*, New York, NY: Routledge 1991, pp. 81–117.
Hipple, F. S., Multinational Companies and International Trade: The Impact of Intrafirm Shipments on US Foreign Trade 1977–1982, *Journal of International Business Studies*, 21, 3, 1990, pp. 495–504.
Hitt, M. A., Hoskisson, R. E. and Kim, H., International Diversification: Effects of Innovation and Firm Performance in Product-Diversified Firms, *Academy of Management Journal*, 40, 4, 1997, pp. 767–798.
Hout, T. M./Porter, M. E./Rudden, E., How Global Companies Win Out, *Harvard Business Review*, 60, 5, 1982, pp. 98–108.
Jaccard, J./Turrisi, R./Wan, C. K., *Interaction Effects in Multiple Regression*, Newbury Park, CA: Sage 1990.
Jensen, M. C., Eclipse of the Public Corporation, *Harvard Business Review*, 67, 5, 1989, pp. 61–74.
Johansson, J. K./Yip, G. S., Exploiting Globalization Potential: US and Japanese Strategies, *Strategic Management Journal*, 15, 8, 1994, pp. 579–601.
Kobrin, S. J., An Empirical Analysis of the Determinants of Global Integration, *Strategic Management Journal*, 12, Summer Special Issue, 1991, pp. 17–31.
Kogut, B./Zander, U., Knowledge of the Firm, Combinative Capabilities, and the Replication of Technology, *Organization Science*, 3, 3, 1992, pp. 383–397.
Kogut, B./Zander, U., Knowledge of the Firm and the Evolutionary Theory of the Multinational Corporation, *Journal of International Business Studies*, 24, 4, 1993, pp. 625–645.
Kotabe, M./Srinivasan, S. S./Aulakh, P. S., Multinationality and Firm Performance: The Moderating Role of R & D and Marketing Capabilities, *Journal of International Business Studies*, 33, 1, 2002, pp. 79–97.
Kutschker, M./Baurle, I., Three Plus One: Multidimensional Strategy of Internationalization, *Management International Review*, 37, 2, 1997, pp. 103–125.
Laverty, K. J., Economic "Short-Termism": The Debate, the Unresolved Issues, and the Implications for Management Practice and Research, *Academy of Management Review*, 21, 3, 1996, pp. 825–860.
Levitt, T., The Globalization of Markets, *Harvard Business Review*, 61, 3, 1983, pp. 92–102.
Levy, D. L., International Sourcing and Supply Chain Stability, *Journal of International Business Studies*, 26, 2, 1995, pp. 343–360.
Malnight, T. W., The Transition from Decentralized to Network-Based MNC Structures: An Evolutionary Perspective, *Journal of International Business Studies*, 27, 1, 1996, pp. 43–65.
Martinez, J. I./Jarillo, J. C., Coordination Demands of International Strategies, *Journal of International Business Studies*, 22, 3, 1991, pp. 429–444.
Mataloni Jr, R. J./Yorgason, D. R., Operations of US Multinational Companies: Preliminary Results from the 1999 Benchmark Survey, *Survey of Current Business*, 82, 3, 2002, pp. 24–54.
Mauri, A. J./Phatak, A. V., Global Integration as Inter-Area Product Flows: The Internalization of Ownership and Location Factors Influencing Product Flows across MNC units, *Management International Review*, 41, 3, 2001, pp. 233–249.

Morck, R./Yeung, B., Why Investors Value Multinationality, *Journal of Business*, 64, 2, 1991, pp. 165–187.
Ohmae, K., *The Borderless World : Power and Strategy in the Interlinked World Economy*, New York, NY: Harper Business 1990.
Palepu, K., Diversification Strategy, Profit Performance and the Entropy Measure, *Strategic Management Journal*, 6, 3, 1985, pp. 239–255.
Pfeffer, J./Salancik, G. R., *The External Control of Organizations: A Resource Dependency Perspective*, New York: Harper and Row 1978.
Porter, M. E., Competition in Global Industries: A Conceptual Framework, in Porter, M. E. (ed), *Competition in Global Industries*, Boston, MA: Harvard Business School Press 1986, pp. 15–60.
Prahalad, C. K./Doz, Y. L., *The Multinational Mission: Balancing Local Demands and a Global Vision*, New York: The Free Press 1987.
Roth, K., Managing International Interdependence: CEO Characteristics in a Resource-Based Framework, *Academy of Management Journal*, 38, 1, 1995, pp. 200–231.
Roth, K./Morrison, A. J., An Empirical Analysis of the Integration-Responsiveness Framework in Global Industries, *Journal of International Business Studies*, 21, 4, 1990, pp. 541–564.
Roth, K./Morrison, A. J., Implementing Global Strategy: Characteristics of Global Subsidiary Mandates, *Journal of International Business Studies*, 23, 4, 1992, pp. 715–735.
Sambharya, R. B./Phatak, A., The Effect of Transborder Data Flow Restrictions on American Multinational Corporations, *Management International Review*, 30, 3, 1990, pp. 267–289.
Scherer, F. M./Ross, D., *Industrial Market Structure and Economic Performance*, Princeton, NJ: Houghton Mifflin 1990.
Stopford, J. M./Wells, L. T., *Managing the Multinational Enterprise: Organization of The Firm and Ownership of the Subsidiaries*, New York, NY: Basic Books 1972.
Takeuchi, H./Porter, M. E., Three Roles of International Marketing in Global Strategy, in Porter, M. E. (ed), *Competition in Global Industries*, Boston: Harvard Business School Press 1986, pp. 111–146.
Tallman, S./Li, J., Effects of International Diversity and Product Diversity on the Performance of Multinational firms, *Academy of Management Journal*, 39, 1, 1996, pp. 179–196.
Teece, D., Transactions Cost Economics and the Theory of the Multinational Enterprise, *Journal of Economic Behavior and Organization*, 7, 1986, pp. 21–45.
Thompson, J. D., *Organizations in Action*, New York: McGraw-Hill 1967.
Tushman, M. L./Nadler, D. A., Information Processing as an Integrating Concept in Organizational Design, *Academy of Management Review*, 3, 3, 1978, pp. 613–624.
Wernerfelt, B., A Resource-Based View of the Firm, *Strategic Management Journal*, 5, 2, 1984, pp. 171–180.
Zeile, W. J., US Intrafirm Trade in Goods, *Survey of Current Business*, 77, 2, 1997, pp. 23–38.
Zeile, W. J., US Affiliates of Foreign Companies: Operation in 1999, *Survey of Current Business*, 81, 8, 2001, pp. 141–158.

mir *Edition*

Jörg Frehse

International Service Competencies

Strategies for Success in the European Hotel Industry

2002, XXVI, 353 pages, pb., € 59,00 (approx. US $ 59,–)
ISBN 3-409-12349-0

European hotels, which tend to be individual businesses, have a hard time resisting the continued globalization pressure. In order to survive the fierce international competition, Europe's hotel business needs to offer their potential customers an added value that they do not receive from hotel chains. The author shows how European individual hotels can prevail by developing international service competencies.

The book is addressed to lecturers and students of economics, in particular in the field of management and tourism, as well as managers and consultants in the hotel and tourist industry.

Betriebswirtschaftlicher Verlag Dr. Th. Gabler GmbH, Abraham-Lincoln-Str. 46, 65189 Wiesbaden

Niels G. Noorderhaven/Anne-Wil Harzing

The "Country-of-origin Effect" in Multinational Corporations: Sources, Mechanisms and Moderating Conditions

Abstract

- This conceptual paper examines the role of country-of-origin effects in MNCs. It deals with definitional problems and discusses both the sources of the country-of-origin effect, and the mechanisms through which it manifests itself.

- The strength of the country-of-origin effect is hypothesized to be moderated by factors related to both the home country and the MNC.

Key Results

- The sources of the effect lie in the culture and institutions of the home country of the MNC. The mechanisms through which the effect manifests itself are the (continued) hiring of home-country nationals by the MNC, and the expression of the administrative preferences of these home-country nationals in the organizational structures, procedures and processes of the MNC.

- The homogeneity of the home culture, substantive characteristics of the home-country culture, the size and openness of the home-country economy, the cultural and institutional diversity of the environments in which the MNC operates, and the international growth path of the MNC are proposed to impact on the strength of the country-of-origin effect.

Authors

Dr. Niels G. Noorderhaven, Professor of International Management, Tilburg University, The Netherlands.
Dr. Anne-Wil Harzing, Senior Lecturer in International Management, Department of Management, University of Melbourne, Australia.

Introduction

Globalization is assumed to bring about a process of convergence of cultural, political and economic aspects of life (Giddens 1999). In the globalization debate the multinational corporation (MNC) is often presented as a harbinger of global practices (Dicken 1998). As knowledge is assumed to move more easily within than across organizational boundaries (Buckley/Casson 1985, Bartlett/Ghoshal 1989), MNCs operating in many different countries can be expected to speed up the international harmonization of technologies and organizational practices (Mueller 1994). While practices rooted in local idiosyncrasies may survive in local firms, within MNCs international 'best practices' are expected to disseminate more quickly. At the same time, however, students of the MNC are increasingly recognizing the complexity and internal differentiation of this type of organization. As subsidiaries play different roles within the MNC and are faced with divergent local institutional, cultural and economic conditions, it stands to reason that these subsidiaries are not only internally differentiated, but are also managed in different ways by the MNC headquarters (Martinez/Jarillo 1991, Nohria/Ghoshal 1997, Harzing 1999). Furthermore, even though business may become increasingly global in many respects, the MNC remains dependent upon certain local environments for its competitive advantages and renewal thereof (Sölvell/Zander 1995).

This view of the MNC casts doubt on the presumed role of these firms in the globalization process, as far as the international transfer and harmonization of technologies and practices is concerned. Moreover, the view that whatever is transferred by the MNC to its subsidiaries can indeed be assumed to be international 'best practice' is increasingly questioned. Far from being 'nationless' organizations, as suggested by Ohmae (1990), even the most global MNCs in many respects still appear to be strongly rooted in their country-of-origin (Hu 1992, Ruigrok/Van Tulder 1995). A small but growing body of literature discusses this 'country-of-origin' effect in MNCs (for overviews, see Ferner 1997 and Harzing/Sorge 2003). Pauly and Reich (1997), looking at MNCs from the United States, Japan, and Germany, conclude that the behavior of the firms studies divides into three distinct 'syndromes', typical of the respective national origins; and that these 'syndromes are durably nested in broader domestic institutional and ideological structures' (Pauly/Reich 1997, p. 24). Ngo et al. (1998) studied the effect of the nationality of the parent company on human resource practices of subsidiaries operating in Hong Kong. Comparing these practices for subsidiaries with parent firms from the United States, Great Britain, Japan, and Hong Kong itself, they find strong support for the hypothesis that country-of-origin influences the firms' human resource management practices (Ngo et al. 1998, p. 642). Lubatkin et al. (1998) focus on the administrative approach used by headquarters in recently acquired subsidiaries in Britain and France. During the transition period following an acquisition, the initial control strategies employed by the parent firm are seen as reflecting the acquiring firm's beliefs about 'how things ought to be done' (Lubatkin et al. 1998, p. 671). They conclude that British and French parent firms tend to establish different headquarters-subsidiary relationships, with the French acquiring firms being more inclined to transfer managers to key positions in the acquired firms than British acquiring firms, and also exerting higher levels of centralized control (Lubatkin et al. 1998, p. 679–680). Most recently, based on data on 287 subsidiaries from 104 MNCs, Harzing and Sorge (2003) conclude that country-of-origin comes forward as one of the most important predictors of the control mechanisms used by MNCs, while also influencing their overall internationalization strategy to some extent. Likewise, Harzing, Sorge, and Pauwe (2002) find large differences between German and British MNCs in nearly all aspects of the headquarters-subsidiary relationship.

To the extent that the country-of-origin effect is significant, the influence of MNCs in the globalization process becomes ambivalent, and in internal MNC exchanges MNC headquarters cannot properly be regarded to be representing the 'global' and subsidiaries the 'local'. On the other hand, not all the evidence points in the same direction. Tregaskis (1998) conducted an analysis comparable to that of Ngo et al. (1998) for firms operating in Britain, comparing nationally owned companies with subsidiaries of MNCs from continental Europe, the United States, and Japan. But in contrast with Ngo et al. (1998), she found only limited differences in human resource development practices associated with the parent company's national origin. Likewise, Lindholm (1999–2000) found that the European MNC he studied adopted standardized performance management policies and practices both in its home country and in overseas subsidiaries, and that these policies and practices had a broadly similar impact on the job satisfaction of host-country employees in different subsidiaries. Hayden and Edwards (2001), although stating that 'MNCs continue to be firmly embedded in, and strongly influenced by, their country of origin' (p. 132), nevertheless observed that the country-of-origin effect in a large Swedish MNC eroded as foreign, mainly Anglo-Saxon, practices were adopted.

Hence, although there is significant evidence of the existence of a country-of-origin effect on MNCs, there are also conflicting findings, and it seems that there are many factors influencing both the manner in which the effect manifests itself and its strength. This is not surprising, since – as we will expound below – there are many factors at different levels that have to be taken into account, and these factors may be assumed to interact in complex ways. In this paper we aim to unravel the complex set of factors associated with the country-of-origin effect on MNCs by looking at the sources of the effect, the mechanisms through which it affects the MNC and its subsidiaries, and the conditions that moderate the effect. Such an analysis can help future research to delimit the country-of-origin effect more clearly, and in doing so become more cumulative.

In order to keep complexity within bounds, the next section will first provide our reasoned interpretation of the country-of-origin effect, and we will restrict our further discussion to the effect delineated in this way. After that, we discuss the sources of the effect, as well as the mechanisms through which it impacts on the MNC and its subsidiaries. Finally, based on this discussion of sources and mechanisms, we focus on the conditions that moderate the country-of-origin effect, since an explanation for previous, sometimes conflicting findings, may well be that the strength with which the country-of-origin effect manifests itself depends on a set of factors which are not invariant across studies. Our discussion leads to a number of propositions regarding the strength of the country-of-origin effect that can offer guidance to further research in this area. Conclusions follow.

Definition of the Country-of-origin Effect

The country-of-origin effect so far remains ill-defined. As a consequence, authors discuss widely diverging phenomena as examples of the effect, and in their explanations refer to very different mechanisms producing the effect. In order to streamline our discussion, we will have to delineate our understanding of the country-of-origin effect. In this respect, we will discuss two important distinctions: the distinction between phenomena at the level the individual subsidiaries and phenomena at the level of the MNC as a whole, and the distinction between the effect of deliberate policies of the MNC and that of subconscious influences.

Firstly, regarding the distinction between subsidiary-level and MNC-level phenomena, there is an abundance of research indicating the existence of important differences between subsidiaries of the same MNC (Ghoshal/Nohria 1989, Martinez/Jarillo 1991, Harzing 1999). These differences can be caused by adaptation to local circumstances, differences in the roles played by the subsidiaries within the MNC, differences in size or age of the subsidiaries, differences in their origins (start-up versus acquisition), as well as overall MNC policies, to name just a few. If we don't clarify whether the country-of-origin effect pertains to the overall policy of the MNC or to characteristics of the subsidiaries, we run the risk of falling into circular explanations, in which the country-of-origin effect is seen as influencing itself. Arguably, the level of complexity is highest at the level of the subsidiaries, since units at this level have to deal with 'a multitude of different and possibly conflicting institutional pressures' (Kostova/Roth 2002, p. 215). Therefore, we restrict our definition of the country-of-origin effect to phenomena at the level of the MNC as a whole, realizing that the extent to and the way in which these phenomena make themselves felt at the subsidiary level depend on many factors we cannot control for. More specifically, we limit ourselves to the influence of country of origin on two related sets of phenomena at the MNC level: the internationalization strategy and the international control strategy of the MNC. The concept of 'internationalization strategies' refers to the way in which the MNC models relationships between headquarters and subsidiaries, as well as with the markets and institutional context they operate in (Harzing/Sorge 2003). Based on the seminal work of Bartlett and Ghoshal (1989), the two main dimensions in which internationalization strategies differ can be said to be the responsiveness to local markets and other local factors and the extent of global integration. The concept of 'international control strategy' refers to the mechanisms the MNC uses to achieve coordination and alignment between its many units. Here the main dimensions are the directness and explicitness of control on the one hand, and the impersonality of control on the other (Harzing 1999).

There are many other phenomena in MNCs that could be claimed to be subject to country-of-origin effects, such as human resource policies, industrial relations, or the communication systems (see Ferner 1997, Bomers/Peterson 1977, and Nobel/Birkinshaw 1998, respectively). We have chosen for two broad categories of potential country-of-origin effects repositories because they represent two important and related aspects of MNCs at two different levels of policy generality. The internationalization strategy reflects fundamental choices concerning what type of MNC the company wants to be (Bartlett/Ghoshal 1989). One would expect the international control strategy to be partly determined by the internationalization strategy, but Harzing and Sorge (2003) show that companies appear to have a lot of leeway in fashioning their control strategy, even within a particular internationalization strategy. The international control strategy may, in turn, be expected to exert a relatively strong influence on lower-level phenomena in which country-of-origin effects may be expressed (Tregaskis 1998). The internationalization strategy and the international control strategy represent the most 'international' and potentially most decontextualized aspects of the MNC (Harzing/Sorge 2003). If country-of-origin effects can be found here, there is strong evidence that these effects do indeed remain relevant in spite of globalization.

Secondly, as mentioned above, we are of the opinion that we should distinguish between the effects of deliberate decisions and subconscious influences. Both can lead to home-country specific characteristics of MNCs. For instance, Pauly and Reich (1997) refer, among other things, to the decisions of MNCs to invest in R & D facilities at geographical locations outside of the home country, and find significant differences between American, Japanese and German MNCs in this respect. The step to invest in R & D facilities at a specific locality clearly is the result of a deliberate decision, presumably taking into account objective factors regarding the comparative attractiveness of potential localities. Other occurrences of home-country specific effects, however, may be expected to be much less subject to deliberate decision making. This appears to be true for the control strategies used by MNCs. Lubatkin et al. (1998, p. 671) see organization members' beliefs about 'how things ought to be' as the source for the country-of-origin effects they identified, and quote Nonaka's (1994) reference to judgments that 'transcend factual or pragmatic considerations' in assent. We think that an explanation of country-of-origin effects should concentrate on this type of effects, as this seems to us to be the more 'pure' type, uncontaminated by deliberations that have to do more with contingency factors that happen to differ between countries, than with country-of-origin effects as such.

Sethi and Elango's (1999) conceptual paper about country-of-origin effects on MNC strategies does not make this distinction. The authors put forward a concept of country-of-origin effects comprising three elements: '(1) economic and physical resources and industrial capabilities; (2) cultural values and institutional norms; and (3) national government's economic and industrial policies' (Sethi/Elango 1999, p. 287). To combine three so radically different factors in a single concept of 'country-of-origin effects' seems counterproductive. This effect should rather be isolated from contingency effects and policies of national governments (the first and third categories mentioned by Sethi and Elango), in order to more accurately gauge its effect. Meshing factors that are subject to deliberate decision-making and choice and factors that are not, Sethi and Elango come to talk not only about 'a firm's choice of international competitive strategies and operational modes', but also of a firm that 'takes cognizance of ... cultural values and norms and patterns its organizational structure and operational practices so as to maximize the beneficial aspects of these norms' (Sethi/Elango 1999, p. 287 and p. 291, respectively). In our view, the second quote is symptomatic of a view in which culture and institutions are just another set of factors the MNC will have to take into consideration in determining its policy. In contrast, we adhere to the view that culture and (to a lesser extent) national institutions influence MNC behavior not primarily because they are deliberately factored into a decision equation, but rather through tacit beliefs and implicit values of its key decision makers. This view of the country-of-origin effect fits in with the sources of the effect and the mechanisms through which it operates, discussed in the next section.

To summarize: we restrict our analysis of the country-of-origin effect on MNCs to phenomena at the level of the MNC as a whole, notably the internationalization strategy and the international control strategy of the MNC, and we focus on the undeliberate influence of factors related to the culture and institutions of the home country. A possible criticism of this approach could be that there is a tension between the focus on undeliberate influences and the selection of internationalization strategy and international control strategy as main elements in which the effect manifests itself. However, it seems impossible to completely isolate subconscious effects from those produced by deliberate decision making. We contend that both the internationalization strategy and the international control strategy of an MNC are partly the result of deliberate decisions by MNC management, in response to objective factors in the environment, and partly the result of choices made by the same management, but on the basis of largely subconscious beliefs and values. This means that if we want to measure the country-of-origin effect, we will always have to control for all relevant contingency factors.

Diagram 1 clarifies the conceptual model underlying our definition of the country-of-origin effect. Internationalization strategies are assumed to be influenced by both contingency factors in the task environment, and the country-of-origin of the MNC. The contingency factors differ between industries, and cause particular internationalization strategies to be more popular in some industries than in others. However, the choice of an internationalization strategy could also be influenced by the country of origin of the MNC (Dowling/Welch/Schuler 1999, Sölvell/Zander 1995). The international control strategy may be assumed to be influenced by the internationalization strategy, as some internationalization strategies ask for more control, or control of a different kind, than others (Harzing 1999). However, we cannot rule out the possibility that the international control strategy is also directly influenced by contingency factors, such as for instance size or industry (Harzing/Sorge 2003). Hence, in analyzing the country-of-origin effect on international control strategies we will have to control for both internationalization strategy and factors in the task environment of the MNC.

Diagram 1. Conceptual Model of Country-of-Origin Effects

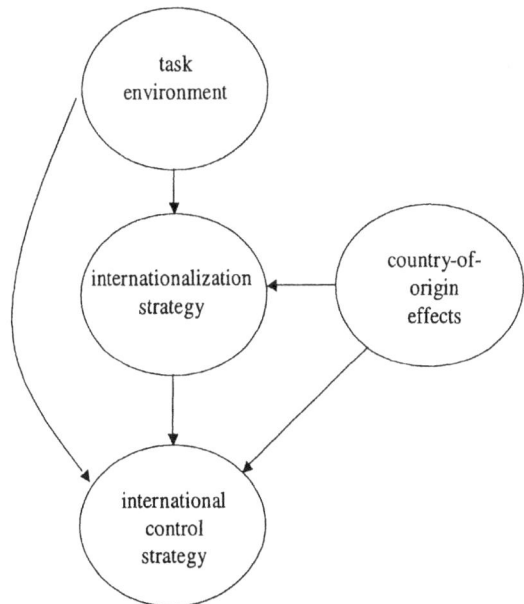

Based on the discussion above, we adopt the following definition of the country-of-origin effect for the purpose of the analysis in this paper:

The country-of-origin effect consists of that part of the differences in internationalization strategies and international control strategies of MNCs that can be ascribed to the different national origins of these MNCs, rather than to variations in their task environment.

One final issue needs clarification: what country can be assumed to be the 'country of origin' of an MNC? This is not necessarily given by the location of MNC headquarters, as this may be relocated for, for instance, tax reasons at a moment at which the internationalization strategy and international control strategy are already formed. Rather, the country-of-origin is determined by its 'historical experience and the institutional and ideological legacies of that experience' (Pauly/Reich 1997, p. 4), i.e., the country in which the MNC 'grew up' is important. As most MNCs have initially started to operate within national borders, this criterion should not pose too many problems. The only exceptions would be MNCs that at an early stage acquired a bi-national status (e.g., Shell), MNCs that are the result of an international merger and have since developed into a new entity (e.g., ABB) or MNCs that could be classified as born global firms (Bell/McNaughton/Young 2001). The following discussion applies to those MNCs that have a clear single country of origin.

Sources and Mechanisms of Operation of the Country-of-origin Effect

Differences between countries that can give rise to country-of-origin effects are well-documented in the international comparative management literature. The literature can be divided into two schools of thought: the culturalist and the institutionalist orientation. The culturalist tradition leans heavily on the work of Geert Hofstede, and in particular the indices of national value dimensions he developed (Hofstede 1980, 2001). The underlying assumption is that individuals become 'mentally programmed' by the way they are raised by their parents and peers and by the institutions (in particular the educational institutions) in the country in which they grow up. This makes them adopt broad preferences for certain states of affairs that they share, to a certain extent, with other people that have grown up under comparable circumstances. For the study of management and organization Hofstede's dimensions of power distance and uncertainty avoidance are most relevant. Power distance is related to preferences regarding the distribution of authority, uncertainty avoidance to the importance of rules and procedures.

In the culturalist perspective, managers from a large power-distance culture will be inclined to centralize decision making, and their subordinates will allow them to do so. Managers from strong uncertainty avoiding cultures will be inclined to use formal rules and procedures to coordinate the activities within the firm, and employees will tend to take these seriously (Hofstede 2001). There is a wealth of studies demonstrating that issues such as leadership and management, centralization of authority, organizational role ambiguity, and authority relations correlate significantly with one or more of Hofstede's cultural indices (see the references in Hofstede 2001). These behaviors are typically not the result of a deliberate evaluation of the pros and cons of various courses of action, but are regarded the natural thing to do: 'Because our values are programmed early in our lives, they are non-rational (although we may subjectively feel our own to be perfectly rational!)' (Hofstede 2001, p. 6). Values guide the selection and justification of actions, the evaluation of people and events, and the social construction of reality.

The institutionalist school sees the institutional environment as the key determinant of organizational characteristics (DiMaggio/Powell 1991, Scott 1995). Three aspects of institutions are distinguished, regulative aspects, as institutions set, monitor and enforce rules; normative aspects, as institutions prescribe desirable goals and the appropriate means of attaining them; and cognitive aspects, as institutions influence the beliefs of actors (Scott 1995). In the field of international comparative management the institutionalist approach is exemplified by, among others, the 'business systems' approach (Whitley 1992a, Whitley/Kristensen 1996). This approach is based on the conviction that differences in the structure and operations of firms from different countries 'clearly stem from variations in dominant social institutions such as the state and the financial systems' (Whitley 1992b, p. 1). In later work, Whitley expanded the range of institutions considered with 'cultural conventions' and the 'labour system' (Whitley 1996, p. 51). Variations in the institutional features of countries are linked to characteristics of economic actors in complex ways, spelled out in many examples in this strongly descriptive literature. A school of thought related to the business systems approach, and chronologically preceding it, is the societal effect approach (Maurice 1979, Maurice/Sorge/ Warner 1980, Sorge/Warner 1986). While focussing on a narrower range of countries in its empirical applications (most studies compare France, Germany and Great Britain), the societal effect approach studies the mechanisms through which institutions imprint the firms operating in a country in more detail. The societal effect approach started with a comparison of wage differentials in Germany and France, and gradually broadened to work organization, qualification systems, organizational structures, etc., summarized in the concept of 'organizational form'. Organizational forms can be functionally equivalent, meaning that various organizational forms can function equally well under a given set of environmental conditions (Sorge 1995). This leaves open the possibility that organizational forms are selected on the basis of their correspondence with societal institutions.

Both the culturalist and the institutionalist approach have tended to focus on the cross-national comparison of purely local or domestic firms, thereby limiting their relevance for cross-national management issues. The pertinent question in the context of this paper is how local culture and institutions of the country of origin impact on MNC policies, in particular internationalization and international control strategies. Through what mechanisms could these sources of local idiosyncrasy exert influence on the MNC?

First of all, as indicated above, almost all MNCs can be associated with one particular country of origin that influenced them during the period that they were not yet extensively internationalized. In these early years, the MNC may be assumed to have been influenced in a way and to an extent comparable to a purely domestic firm. However, in order for a country-of-origin effect to be present, we need to assume this influence is lasting. One approach would be to assume 'hysteresis', or 'a lagging effect after a causal force has been removed' (Pauly/Reich 1997, p. 5). Corporate inertia could cause MNCs to continue behave in ways that were attuned to their cultural and institutional environment as long as they were operating within their country of origin, but that are not necessarily so when operating in an international environment. Although corporate inertia is an important element in any explanation of consistency in firm behavior, we think a satisfactory explanation of the country-of-origin effect has to go beyond that.

As stated earlier, we focus on country-of-origin effects working through subconscious choices influenced by cultural and institutional characteristics of the country in which the decision makers grew up. In doing so, we subscribe, with Ghoshal and Nohria (1989, p. 334) to the view that the cognitive orientations of senior managers are key to understanding the organizational processes through which MNCs adapt themselves to their environment. After all, cultural and institutional elements enter organizations through the people working in them (Kostova/Roth 2002, p. 218). However, in contrast to Ghoshal and Nohria (1989), we also explicitly focus on non-rational influences. Managers may seek to adapt the MNC to its environment, but their view as to how this should be done is colored by the cultural and institutional characteristics of the society in which they were raised. In this we follow Calori et al. (1997).

According to Calori et al. (1997), the 'administrative heritage' of a country is historically influenced by the industrialization process, the system of government, dominant philosophies and religions, and geographic and demographic conditions. Historical events and processes give shape to institutions, which in turn influence the national culture. Building on the business systems approach Calori et al. (1997) distinguish between 'proximate institutions' which tend to have a coercive influence on management practices, such as legal regulations regarding corporate governance, and 'background institutions' such as the family, schools, and religious organizations. Schools are assumed to play a particularly important role in the transmission of cultural values. The primary socialization that people from a particular country receive at school strongly influences their administrative behavior later in life. On the basis of studies of the French and British educational systems, Calori et al. (1997, p. 687) conclude that 'the science and social values that are explicitly and implicitly communicated at schools in France (...) are different from that which is communicated at comparable British schools. Specifically, the French learn to construct reality in terms of orderly hierarchies, while the British learn to do so in a less controlling, more individualistic way'. Comparable analyses are made of the religious and family systems of the two countries.

While endorsing the approach followed by Calori et al. (1997), we believe that an explanation on the basis of values instilled by institutions such as the family, schools, and religion, melts into the culturalist approach. The culturalist and the institutionalist approach seem to be complementary, as neither the concept of culture nor that of institutions alone captures the full spectrum of national differences that are important for the MNC (Xu/Shenkar 2002). However, we prefer to reserve the term 'institution' for more formal arrangements, such as legislation, and the term 'culture' for informal institutions and forms of influence, such as typical child-raising practices and typical career patterns. Obviously there is overlap between the two concepts, but the influence of the 'background institutions' described by Calori et al. (1997) can be effectively gauged with previously identified dimensions of culture, whereas that of the 'proximate institutions' appears to be less susceptible to this type of measurement. We will return to this issue in the next section.

Given that the country-of-origin effect is assumed to work through the administrative behavior of country-of-origin nationals working for the MNC, a prime mechanism for a permanent (or at least durable) country-of-origin effect is the continued hiring of country-of-origin nationals, even when the firm is operating internationally. Of course, it is not necessary – and not very well conceivable – that the MNC exclusively hires nationals from its country of origin. It suffices if key management positions are dominated by home-country natives. According to Ferner (1997, p. 19), senior management positions continue to be staffed 'disproportionally – often overwhelmingly – by home country nationals'. This continued hiring of home-country nationals for key management positions is the first mechanism through which the country-of-origin effect is preserved.

Secondly, the administrative preferences of the home-country nationals that traditionally have shaped the MNC – and still in many cases dominate top management – will become embedded in organizational structures, procedures, and processes. Organizational structure can be seen as the crystallization of the power relations within the corporation (Pfeffer/Salancik 1978). Both organizational structure and culture embody strategies of the past, and are very difficult to change (Johnson 1988). When the company starts to expand abroad it will tend to use the same structures, etc., in managing its foreign activities; MNCs may be fairly 'ethnocentric' in this regard (Jain/Lawler/Morishima 1998, p. 566). The international application of nationally-inherited administrative approaches can be effected both through formal and informal procedures and through the influence of expatriates (Tregaskis 1998). Presumably, the tendency to use home-grown administrative practices for international operations will to a certain extent be counterbalanced by other forces, calling for either more diversity of practices or for a dominant practice that is different from that of the country-of-origin (Ghoshal/Nohria 1989, Kostova/Roth 2002). So increasing internationalization of the firm will be likely to lead to some extent of adaptation of the way in which it is managed. In this sense the country-of-origin effect as it can be found in a truly international MNC can be seen as a residual of its history. But, assuming continued hiring of home-country nationals for key management positions and embedding of administrative preferences in organizational structures, procedures and processes, this may be expected to be a particularly persistent residual, and hence the country-of-origin effect should be given due attention in studying the management of MNCs.

Moderating Conditions of the Country-of-origin Effect

If the analysis of the origin and mechanisms of the country-of-origin effect in the previous sections is correct, the question remains why – as indicated in the introduction – in some studies this effect comes out much stronger than in others. We believe that this is caused by a number of factors that influence the existence and strength of the country-of-origin effect. Further progress in the study of the effect depends crucially on taking these influences into account. This section will discuss the circumstances under which the country-of-origin effect may be expected to be stronger or weaker, and we will formulate propositions regarding the directions of these effects to guide future research. These propositions pertain to the country-of-origin effect as it has been defined earlier in the paper, i.e., that part of the differences in internationalization strategies and international control strategies of MNCs that can be ascribed to the different national origins of these MNCs, rather than to variations in their task environment. In order to control for variations in the task environment, any empirical study of the country-of-origin effect on MNCs will have to control for industry membership, as the transmission of home-country influence will be more marked in industries in which operating units are more integrated into the international corporate strategy of the parent (Ferner 1997). In the propositions formulated below, the *ceterus paribus* clause is assumed to apply as far as industry membership is concerned.

We will discuss the effect of three categories of moderators of the country-of-origin effect: culture, institutions, and contingencies (in as far as they are not covered by industry membership), both at the level of the home country and at the level of the MNC. Hence we distinguish six categories of moderators (see Table 1).

Table 1. Moderators of the Country-of-Origin Effect

	Culture	Institutions	Contingencies
Home Country factors	Homogeneity of home-country culture (proposition 1a) Characteristics of home-country culture (proposition 1b)	Characteristics of home-country institutional regime (no proposition)	Size of home country economy (proposition 2a) Openness of home country economy (proposition 2b)
MNC-specific factors	Cultural diversity of environments in which the MNC operates (proposition 3)	Diversity of institutional regimes in which MNC operates (proposition 4)	International growth path of MNC (proposition 5)

Home-Country Factors

The culture of the home country of the MNC may be expected to moderate the strength of the country-of-origin effect. We expect a stronger, i.e., more homogenous national culture in the country of origin to lead to stronger country-of-origin effects in MNCs originating from that country. The importance of strength of culture has been documented for organizational cultures by Peters and Waterman (1982), who observed that excellent companies are characterized by strong cultures, with shared values forming the core of these cultures. These cultures are 'strong' because, since they are homogenous, there is unity of purpose. The influence on individuals will be very strong as there is little room for divergent behavior. The same mechanism may be expected to be at work at the level of national cultures. In more homogenous national cultures the variety of behaviors is smaller, with the consequence that the culturally approved or permitted ways of doing things, including the management of organizations, is less likely to be questioned. In cultures that are more heterogeneous, culturally transferred practices will be more easily recognized as optional, rather than necessary. Hence:

Proposition 1a. The cultural homogeneity of the home country positively moderates the strength of the country-of-origin effect.

Secondly, particular characteristics of the home country culture (rather than its homogeneity) may be expected to moderate the strength of the country-of-origin effect. Firms from some countries, with certain cultural values, may be better able to adapt to local conditions than firms from other countries (Ngo et al. 1998). Lubatkin et al. (1998) note that the managers from the French firms in their data-set tend to exert much more strategic control than their British counterparts, and they explain this on the basis of the different 'administrative heritages' or cultures of these two countries. Looking at Hofstede's (1980) indices, we note that the two countries differ in particular in the dimensions of power distance and uncertainty avoidance, with France scoring higher on both dimensions. A large power distance, as mentioned earlier, is associated with centralization in management, as found, for instance, by Wong and Birnbaum-More (1994) in a sample of multinational banks. Strong uncertainty avoidance is associated with strict control (see, e.g., Offermann/Hellmann 1997). Without denying the possibility that other dimensions of national culture in some way moderate the country-of-origin effect, we focus on power distance and uncertainty avoidance, as these two dimensions are particularly relevant for the functioning of organizations. (Hofstede 2001, p. 375).

The influence of power distance and uncertainty avoidance on headquarter-subsidiary relations as observed by Lubatkin et al. (1998) can be interpreted in two ways. The relatively 'hands-off' approach of the British acquiring firms can be seen as an expression of the small power-distance, weak uncertainty-avoidance characteristics of the home country culture, and the strong control attitude of the French acquiring firms as an expression of the contrasting characteristics of the French national culture in these respects. While such an interpretation would not a-priori be invalid, it would form the basis of a hypothesis regarding the substantive country-of-origin effects of cultural characteristics of the home country. However, it would not be helpful in understanding why the country-of-origin effect is stronger in some cases than in others, i.e., the moderating effect of the home country culture on the strength of the country-of-origin effect. As we are interested in these moderating factors, we choose to look at the issue from this perspective. Both a large power distance and a strong uncertainty avoidance can reasonably be hypothesized to lead to a tendency to exert strong influence from the home country on the management of subsidiaries overseas. Hence, these dimensions may also be assumed to positively affect the strength of the country-of-origin effect:

Proposition 1b. Home-country cultures that are characterized by a large power distance and/or a strong uncertainty avoidance positively moderate the strength of the country-of-origin effect of MNCs.

Apart from culture, the institutional characteristics of the home country may moderate country-of-origin effects. Kostova (1999) distinguishes three components of 'country institutional profiles': the regulatory component, the cognitive component, and the normative component. The latter two aspects of institutional profiles overlap with culture, but the regulatory component is unique to the concept of institutions (Kostova 1999, p. 314). Dimensionalizing and measuring country institutional profiles may in due time enable the formulation of propositions based on concrete substantive institutional characteristics. However, before that is possible more developmental work on measuring institutional profiles is necessary (Kostova 1997). Busenitz et al. (2000) measure the three dimensions of institutional profiles with questionnaire items. This has the disadvantage, particularly with regard to the regulatory dimension, that it yields very abstract institutional profiles, as respondents' general impressions and perceptions of government policies rather than actual laws and regulations are tapped. Another issue that has to be addressed is the level of specificity that is desirable in measuring country institutional profiles. Kostova (1997) argues that institutional profiles should be measured with regard to specific domains. However, the more specific the measurement of institutional characteristics is to the organizational phenomena studied, the larger the danger of tautological explanations. A strong point of very general societal characteristics (such as Hofstede's dimensions of culture) is that the relationship with organizational phenomena is not self-evident, and hence constitutes a non-trivial finding.

At present, our knowledge of the influence of the institutional profile of the home country on the management of MNCs is insufficient to form the basis of plausible propositions pertaining to substantive characteristics of institutional environments. Whitley (1999), for instance, distinguishes six ideal types of business systems, based on the degree of ownership-based coordination of economic activities, and the extent of non-ownership-based or alliance form of organizational integration. But while the implications of these types of business systems for firms operating within them are analyzed, it remains unclear to what extent these environments differ in the extent to which firms originating from them display a tendency to 'export' home-grown practices to their subsidiaries overseas. This is not to say that the institutions of the home country are assumed not to moderate the country-of-origin effect. To the contrary, such moderating effects are quite likely. For instance, Hayden and Edwards (2001, p. 117) note that the fact that Sweden had a set of highly distinctive institutions for a long time has influenced the country-of-origin effect in Swedish MNCs. But as these authors also note, the differences between the home country institutional environment and that of the host country are also important. German MNCs have been willing to export German-style vocational training in UK subsidiaries because Britain lacks the institutions necessary to underpin these practices (Hayden/Edwards 2001, p. 122). On the basis of these considerations, we do not formulate a proposition pertaining to substantive characteristics of institutional characteristics of the home country and the strength of country-of-origin effects here. We restrict ourselves to differences between institutional environments (see proposition 4 below).

Finally, we discuss two home country contingency variables that might moderate country-of-origin effects: the size and openness of the economy. A smaller and more open economy in the country of origin may lead to weaker country-of-origin effects for MNCs originating from that country. Firms from smaller nations and nations with more open economies have been forced in their history to compete and/or cooperate with foreign companies and to demonstrate adaptability (Pauly/Reich 1997). MNCs from countries such as Sweden or Switzerland, with smaller home markets, are likely to be more 'international' in terms of the proportion of their foreign operations than MNCs from larger countries (Ferner 1997). MNCs originating from small nations also presumably started doing business abroad at an early stage of their development, and hence have acquired the ability to accommodate foreign administrative approaches. If two MNCs are at present internationalized to the same extent, the MNC from a small open economy may be expected to have embarked on the path of internationalization earlier in its history, and hence bear a weaker imprint from the culture and institutions of its home country.

Hence, our propositions:

Proposition 2a. Home countries with small economies negatively moderate the strength of the country-of-origin effect.

Proposition 2b. Home countries with open economies negatively moderate the strength of the country-of-origin effect.

MNC-Specific Factors

Above we have discussed moderating effects of the homogeneity and of specific characteristics of the home-country culture. But culture may also be assumed to play a role in another way. Depending on the set of countries in which they operate, MNCs face different levels of cultural diversity in their environments. The greater the cultural distance between home and host country, the harder it will be for the MNC to transfer home-country philosophies and practices (Ferner 1997). This effect at the level of the single headquarters-subsidiary relationship will presumably also play in an aggregated form at the level of the MNC as a whole. The greater the cultural diversity of the environments the MNC is working in, the weaker the country-of-origin effect in that MNC may be assumed to be. Hence more geographical dispersion will negatively moderate the country-of-origin effect, if this geographical dispersion is across cultures (Hayden/Edwards 2001). Since it becomes more difficult to apply the home-grown administrative approach, MNC-management will become aware of this, and will – perhaps through trial and error – adapt its strategies. The extent of cultural diversity in the MNC's environments is expected to correlate – but imperfectly – with the extent of internationalization of the MNC (see below), as well as the openness and size of the home country economy (see above).

Proposition 3. The level of diversity of the cultural environments in which an MNC operates will negatively moderate the strength of the country-of-origin effect.

Parallel to the predicted moderating effect of aggregated cultural distance, the diversity of institutional environments in which the MNC operates may also be expected to negatively influence the strength of the country-of-origin effect. MNCs working across a diversity of institutional regimes will feel a reduced isomorphic pressure (Xu/Shenkar 2002). Hence:

Proposition 4. The level of diversity of the institutional environments in which an MNC operates will negatively moderate the strength of the country-of-origin effect.

Finally, we propose that the international growth path of the MNC will moderate the strength of country-of-origin effects. MNCs that have historically grown and internationalized through start-ups, rather than acquisitions, are expected to display a stronger country-of-origin effect, since it is easier to install home-grown management practices in new start-ups than in acquired existing firms (Harzing 2002). We could also formulate a proposition pertaining to the overall level of internationalization of the MNC (in terms of sales, production, personnel, or geographical spread of key functions), with the level of internationalization negatively moderating the strength of country-of-origin effects. However, we believe that this effect is already effectively captured by the cumulative cultural and institutional distances, subjects of propositions 3 and 4, respectively. Hence, we restrict ourselves to a single proposition:

Proposition 5. Internationalization through start-ups (rather than acquisitions) will positively moderate the strength of the country-of-origin effect.

Conclusions

There is a growing recognition of the influence of the country-of-origin on important aspects of MNCs. However, empirical findings are not always consistent. This may be caused by the fact that the concept of 'country-of-origin effects' remains ill-defined, and is used by different authors to refer to different aspects of MNCs. It may also be caused by the fact that there are factors moderating the strength of country-of-origin effects that so far have not been identified and adequately incorporated in empirical studies of the effect. In this paper we define the country-of-origin effect as that part of the differences in internationalization strategies and international control strategies of MNCs that can be ascribed to the different national origins of these MNCs, rather than to variations in their task environment. Based on this demarcation, we discuss the sources of the country-of-origin effect, and the mechanisms through which it manifests itself. The sources of the effect are seen to lie in the culture and institutions of the home country of the MNC. The mechanisms through which the effect manifests itself are the (continued) hiring of home-country nationals by the MNC, and the embeddedness of the administrative preferences of these home-country nationals in the organizational structures, procedures and processes of the MNC. The strength of the country-of-origin effect manifested in this way is expected to be moderated by factors related to the home country and to the MNC. The more homogenous the home-country culture, the stronger the country-of-origin effect. A large power distance and/or strong uncertainty avoidance of the home country culture are also expected to positively moderate the strength of the country-of-origin effect. In addition, the size and openness of the home country are expected to be of importance, with smaller and more open home country economies being associated with weaker country-of-origin effects. With regard to the MNC, MNCs operating in a greater diversity of cultural or institutional environments are expected to show weaker country-of-origin effects. Finally, MNCs that have internationalized predominantly though start-ups are expected to show stronger country-of origin effects than MNCs that have grown predominantly through international acquisitions.

The propositions regarding moderators of the country-of-origin effect can form the basis of refutable hypotheses that can be empirically tested. We believe that our understanding of the management of MNCs will be increased through a careful study of country-of-origin effects and the factors moderating these effects. Such knowledge will be theoretically relevant, as it will contribute to an understanding of the role of MNCs in the international transfer of organizational practices. It will also be of practical importance, as the country-of-origin effect, as defined in this article, manifests itself largely undeliberately through decisions by managers that are influenced by taken-for-granted cultural values and institutional influences. Being aware of this type of influences and biases increases the possibility of shaping MNC management to reflect the requirements of the task environment, rather than the historical home country culture and institutions.

References

Bartlett, C. A./Ghoshal, S., *Managing Across Borders, The Transnational Solution*, Boston, MA.: Harvard Business School Press 1989.
Bell, J./McNaughton, R./Young, S., 'Born-again Global' Firms. An Exension to the 'Born Global' Phenomenon, *Journal of International Management*, 7, 2001, pp. 173–189.
Bomers, G. B. J./Peterson, R. B., Multinational Corporations and Industrial Relations: The Case of West Germany and the Netherlands, *British Journal of Industrial Relations*, 15, March 1977, pp. 45–62.
Buckley, P. J./Casson, M., *The Economic Theory of the Multinational Enterprise*, London: Macmillan 1985.

Busenitz, L. W./Gomez, C./Spencer, J. W., Country Institutional Profiles: Unlocking Entrepreneurial Phenomena, *Academy of Management Journal*, 43, 2000, pp. 994–1011.
Calori, R./Lubatkin, M./Very, P./Veiga, J. F., Modelling the Origins of Nationally-Bound Administrative Heritages: A Historical Institutional Analysis of French and British Firms, *Organization Science*, 8, 1997, pp. 681–696.
Dicken, P., *Global Shift: Transforming the World Economy*, London: Paul Chapman 1998.
DiMaggio, P. J./Powell, W. W., Introduction, in Powell, W. W./DiMaggio, P. J. (eds.), *The New Institutionalism in Organizational Analysis*, Chicago: University of Chicago Press 1991, pp. 1–38.
Dowling, P./Welch, D. E./Schuler, R., *International Human Resource Management: Managing People in a Multinational Context*, Cincinnati: South-Western College Publishing 1999.
Ferner, A., Country of Origin Effects and Human Resource Management in Multinational Companies', *Human Resource Management Journal*, 7, 1997, pp. 19–37.
Ghoshal, S./Nohria, N., Internal Differentiation within Multinational Corporations, *Strategic Management Journal*, 10, 1989, pp. 323–337.
Giddens, A., *Runaway World: How Globalization is Reshaping our Lives*, London: Profile Books 1999.
Harzing, A.-W. K., *Managing the Multinationals: An International Study of Control Mechanisms*, Cheltenham: Edward Elgar 1999.
Harzing, A.-W. K., Acquisitions versus Greenfield Investments: International Strategy and Management of Entry Modes, *Strategic Management Journal*, 23, 2002, pp. 211–227
Harzing, A.-W. K./Sorge, A. M./Paauwe, J., HQ-subsidiary Relationships in Multinational Companies: A British-German Comparison, in Geppert, M./Matten, D./Williams, K. (eds.), *Challenges for European Management in a Global Context – Experiences from Britain and Germany*, Basingstoke, London, New York: Palgrave 2002, pp. 96–118.
Harzing, A.-W. K/Sorge, A. M., The Relative Impact of Country-of-origin and Universal Contingencies on Internationalization Strategies and Corporate Control in Multinational Enterprises: World-wide and European Perspectives, *Organization Studies*, 24, 2003, pp. 187–214.
Hayden, A./Edwards, T., The Erosion of the Country of Origin Effect; A Case Study of a Swedish Multinational Company, *Relations Industrielles/Industrial Relations*, 56, 2001, pp. 116–140.
Hofstede, G., *Culture's Consequences. International Differences in Work-Related Values*, London: Sage Publications 1980.
Hofstede, G., *Culture's Consequences, Comparing Values, Behaviors, Institutions and Organizations Across Nations*, second edition, Thousand Oaks: Sage Publications 2001.
Hu, Y.-S., Global or Stateless Corporations are National Firms with International Operations, *California Management Review*, Winter 1992, pp. 107–126.
Jain, H. C./Lawler, J. J./Morishima, M., Multinational Corporations, Human Resource Management and Host-country Nationals, *The International Journal of Human Resource Management*, 9, 1998, pp. 553–566.
Johnson, G., Rethinking Incrementalism, *Strategic Management Journal*, 9, 1988, pp. 75–91.
Kostova, T., Country institutional profile: Concept and Measurement, *Proceedings of the Academy of Management*, 1997, 180–184.
Kostova, T., Transnational Transfer of Organizational Practices: A Contextual Perspective, *Academy of Management Review*, 24, 1999, pp. 308–324.
Kostova, T./Roth, K., Adoption of an Organizational Practice by Subsidiaries of Multinational Corporations: Institutional and Relational Effects, *Academy of Management Journal*, 45, 2002, pp. 215–233.
Lindholm, N., National Culture and Performance Management in MNC Subsidiaries, *International Studies of Management & Organization*, 29, 1999–2000, pp. 45–66.
Lubatkin, M./Calori, R./Very, P./Veiga, J. F., Managing Mergers Across Borders: A Two-Nation Exploration of a Nationally Bound Administrative Heritage, *Organization Science*, 9, 1998, pp. 670–684.
Martinez, J. I./Jarillo, J. C., Coordination Demands of International Strategies, *Journal of International Business Studies*, 22, 1991, pp. 429–444.
Maurice, M., For a Study of "the Societal Effect": Universality and Specificity in Organization Research, in Lammers, C. J./Hickson, D. J. (eds.), *Organizations Alike and Unlike*, London: Routledge 1979, pp. 42–60.

Maurice, M./Sorge, A./Warner, M., Societal Differences in Organizing Manufacturing Units. A Comparison of France, Great Britain and West Germany, *Organization Studies*, 1, 1980, pp. 59–86.
Mueller, F., Societal Effect, Organizational Effect and Globalization, *Organization Studies*, 15, 1994, pp. 407–428.
Ngo, H.-Y./Turban, D./Lau, C.-M./Lui, S.-Y., Human Resource Practices and Firm Performance of Multinational Corporations: Influences of Country Origin, *The International Journal of Human Resource Management*, 9, 1998, pp. 632-652.
Nobel, R./Birkinshaw, J., Innovation in Multinational Corporations: Control and Communication Patterns in International R & D Operations, *Strategic Management Journal*, 9, 1998, pp. 479–496.
Nohria, N./Ghoshal, S., *The Differentiated Network*, San Francisco: Jossey-Bass 1997.
Nonaka, I., A Dynamic Theory of Organizational Knowledge Creation, *Organization Science*, 5, 1994, pp. 14–37.
Offermann, L. R./Hellmann, P. S., Culture's Consequences for Leadership Behavior: National Values in Action, *Journal of Cross-Cultural Psychology*, 28, 1997, pp. 342–351.
Ohmae, K., *The Borderless World: Power and Strategy in the Interlinked Economy*, London: Collins 1990.
Pauly, L. W./Reich, S., National Structures and Multinational Corporate Behavior: Enduring Differences in the Age of Globalization, *International Organization*, 51, 1997, pp. 1–30.
Peters, T. J./Waterman, R. H., Jr., *In Search of Excellence: Lessons from America's Best-Run Companies*, New York: Harper & Row 1982.
Pfeffer, J./Salancik, G. R., *The External Control of Organizations: A Resource Dependence Perspective*, New York: Harper & Row 1978.
Ruigrok, W./Van Tulder, R., *The logic of International Restructuring*, London: Routledge 1995.
Scott, R., *Institutions and Organizations*, Thousand Oaks, CA: Sage 1995.
Sethi, S. P./Elango, B., The Influence of „Country of Origin" on Multinational Corporation Global Strategy: A Conceptual Framework, *Journal of International Management*, 5, 1999, pp. 285–298.
Sölvell, Ö./Zander, I., Organization of the Dynamic Multinational Enterprise: The Home-based and the Heterarchical MNE, *International Studies of Management & Organization*, 25, (1–2), 1995, pp. 17–38.
Sorge, A., Cross-national Differences in Personnel and Organization: Describing and Explaining Variables, in Harzing, A. W. K./Van Ruysseveldt, J., *International Human Resource Management*, London: Sage 1995, pp. 99–123.
Sorge, A./Warner, M., *Comparative Factory Organisation. An Anglo German Comparison of Management and Manpower in Manufacturing*, Aldershot: Gower 1986.
Tregaskis, O., HRD in Foreign MNEs Assessing the Impact of Parent Origin Versus Host Country, Context, *International Studies of Management and Organization*, 28, 1, 1998, pp. 136–163.
Whitley, R., (ed.), *European Business Systems; Firms and Markets in their National Contexts*, London: Sage 1992a.
Whitley, R., Societies, Firms and Markets: The Social Structuring of Business Systems, in Whitley, R., (ed.), *European Business Systems; Firms and Markets in their National Contexts*, London: Sage 1992b, pp. 5–45.
Whitley, R., The Social Construction of Economic Actors: Institutions and Types of Firm in Europe and Other Market Economies, in Whitley, R./Kristensen, P. H. (eds.), *The Changing European Firm; Limits to Convergence*, London: Routledge 1996, pp. 39–66.
Whitley, R., Competing Logics and Units of Analysis in the Comparative Study of Economic Organization, *International Studies of Management & Organization*, 29, 2, 1999, pp. 113–126.
Whitley, R./Kristensen, P. H., (eds.), *The Changing European Firm; Limits to Convergence*, London: Routledge 1996.
Wong, G. Y. Y./Birnbaum-More, P. H., Culture, Context and Structure: A Test on Hong Kong Banks, *Organization Studies*, 15, 1994, pp. 99–123.
Xu, D./Shenkar, O., Institutional Distance and the Multinational Enterprise, *Academy of Management Review*, 27, 2002, pp. 608–618.

Peter J. Buckley/Jeremy Clegg/Hui Tan

The Art of Knowledge Transfer: Secondary and Reverse Transfer in China's Telecommunications Manufacturing Industry[1]

Abstract

This paper extends the theory on knowledge transfer and learning within multinational firms. It provides a theory-building study grounded in the context of the entry and operations of foreign multinational enterprises in the Chinese manufacturing industry.

Key Results

- Our primary research supports the proposition that knowledge transfer is predetermined by entry strategy and the conditions under which this is made. The ownership entry choice may lock foreign firms into constraints from which it is difficult to escape.
- Secondary and reverse knowledge transfer is conditional on the characteristics and success of primary transfer. Local factors such as the goals, aptitude and ability of joint venture partners, as well as global strategy, are crucial.

Authors

Peter J. Buckley, Professor of International Business, Director of the Centre for International Business, Leeds University Business School, and Director of the Institute for Research on Contemporary China, University of Leeds, Leeds, UK.

Jeremy Clegg, Jean Monnet Senior Lecturer in European Integration and International Business Management, Centre for International Business, Leeds University Business School, University of Leeds, Leeds, UK.

Hui Tan, Lecturer in Chinese Business and Management, Centre for International Business, Leeds University Business School, University of Leeds, Leeds, UK.

Peter J. Buckley/Jeremy Clegg/Hui Tan

Introduction

This paper examines knowledge transfer to China. It uses case studies for theory development in an exploration of secondary and reverse knowledge transfer. The paper's key propositions are sequential. (1) The ownership mode of entry (wholly owned subsidiary (WOS) or joint venture (JV) with a Chinese partner) determines the feasible strategy set of the entrant. (2) The strategies selected within the constraints of the Chinese environment must reflect the absorptive capacity of the Chinese unit and the cost of transfer. (3) The nature of the primary knowledge transfer influences secondary and reverse transfer out of the primary affiliate. The paper fills gaps in existing theory by focusing on the process of strategy formation in knowledge transfer and by examining transfers into an emerging economy. This contrasts with the vast majority of studies that are conducted on advanced economies.

We propose a tentative model running from entry to strategy to outcome, depending on the constraints of ownership, cost and feasibility in Chinese conditions. Our paper's primary objective is to develop new conceptualisation and insight into the transfer of knowledge into and out of foreign invested enterprises (FIEs) in China. This theory-building exercise is conducive to further testing and suggestive of future empirical developments.

In our model, reverse knowledge transfer occurs when new knowledge is returned to a parent firm. This indicates corporate integration within the MNE on a regional or a global scale. Secondary knowledge transfer can be defined as the transfer of knowledge from the primary affiliate of the foreign investor to a secondary affiliate, that is, one controlled by the primary affiliate. Secondary transfer to further affiliates represents extension or deepening of the reach of the global system of the firm. The transfer of knowledge, technology in particular, in a wide range of sectors has been a major objective of the Chinese government, along with securing foreign capital, in return for which foreign firms are afforded local market access (Engardio/Roberts/Symonds 1996). This principle has remained intact since the inception of the Open Door Policy in December 1978. What has changed, however, is the means through which these objectives have been pursued. In the early years of the Policy, in most sectors, MNEs were unable to invest in China except via an international joint venture (IJV) with a Chinese partner (Roehrig 1994). The IJV was the legally required form of FIE. It offered the opportunity for a Chinese industrial partner to acquire technical knowledge, and satisfied the political imperative for Chinese interests to maintain effective control over industry in China. Discriminatory treatment and excess transaction costs arising from bureaucracy and the economic environment have caused FIEs difficulty in operating profitably (Studwell 2002).

This paper explores secondary and reverse knowledge transfer using two case study firms, Motorola (China) and Shanghai Bell. Their main respective areas of business are mobile and fixed line telephone equipment. In the fixed line telecommunications equipment industry the government can provide market access through its monopsony power. Until mid 2002 the incumbent national network operator (China Telecom) was a monopolist in fixed line services, and it will remain dominant under the latest reform proposals (Financial Times 2002a). Under the joint venture law, market access could be exchanged for FIEs' knowledge and capital transfer. Latterly, the joint venture requirement has been abolished for much of manufacturing (Lemoine 2000, Luo 2000). In the more recent mobile equipment market, access is provided through the freedom to compete in both industrial and consumer segments.

Theoretical Review

The purpose of this review is twofold. First, to formulate theoretical questions based on the existing literature. Second, to identify gaps or inconsistencies in respect of which the cases can be harnessed to generate further theoretical propositions.

Our definition of knowledge is broad. It encompasses more than simply the notion of technology, since other forms of knowledge are likely to accompany this transfer. Knowledge refers to the tacit or explicit understanding in a firm about the relationships between phenomena, structured in a more or less scientific manner (Hedlund/Nonaka 1993, p. 121). It is embodied in routines for the performance of business operations (Nelson/Winter 1982, p. 99), in organisational structures and processes, and in embedded beliefs and behaviour. Knowledge transfer refers to knowledge communicated from one agent to another, such as from one individual to another, or from a group to an entire organisation (Hedlund/Nonaka 1993, p. 123).

To date, research has concentrated on primary knowledge transfer from headquarters to foreign affiliates. This one-way transfer was characterised in the Hymer-Kindleberger approach to the MNE (Hymer 1960 and 1976, Kindleberger 1969) and the product life cycle model (Vernon 1966). However, the MNE of today, as opposed to the stereotypical ethnocentric multinational of the 1950s and 1960s, is rarely engaged in simple uni-directional transfer (Hedlund 1986, Pearce 1989). Chang and Rosenzweig (1995) foresee the affiliate's eventual development to the point where it will have newly developed knowledge and capabilities to transfer. This evolution, while plausible, is not a prescription. Local influences on strategy are taken up in the literature on organisational learning, reviewed below.

Business Strategy, Knowledge Transfer and Organisational Learning

There is a division in the literature between research on organisational learning and that on knowledge transfer, and its offspring, knowledge management (Easterby-Smith/Crossan/Nicolini 2000). This has produced a disjunction that separates the body of work concerned primarily with the creation of new knowledge throughout an organisation from that focusing on the re-use of knowledge generated centrally.

The model for the re-use of existing knowledge within the multinational enterprise dates from the earliest industrial organisation writings on the theory of the MNE (Hymer 1960 and 1976, Kindleberger 1969, Magee 1977a and 1977b). This portrays the foreign investor as enjoying an absolute firm-specific advantage over host country firms. Production is organised vertically, with knowledge creation concentrated in the home country and horizontal diversification in the hosts. In this account, barriers to knowledge transfer create transaction costs which, if greater in external markets (inter-firm transfer) than in internal markets (intra-firm transfer), promote the choice of the multinational enterprise as an organisational form (Buckley/Casson 1976).

However, if it is the aim of the firm to develop new products, whatever the market or location, then a strategy for knowledge creation is needed. This approach benefits from a "learning network" of people (Tempest 1999) that is not necessarily related to the formal organisational systems and structures of the organisation, nor indeed to the formal boundaries of the firm. This social constructionist view redraws the map of the firm's knowledge creation activity (Davenport/De Long/Beers 1998, Ruggles 1998). This accounts for the current interest in the role of the local embeddedness of the firm in the creation of new knowledge.

Both knowledge re-use and knowledge creation are important (Hansen/Nohria/Tierney 1999). When the firm's business strategy is primarily to replicate existing products in new markets or production locations re-use is optimal. Thus a codification strategy is ideal, whereby knowledge is recorded for access by the knowledge recipients. This might be in the form of knowledge objects in databases or libraries as part of a "people-to-documents" knowledge management strategy. When a knowledge creation strategy is implemented, personalisation is more appropriate. This is described as a "people-to-people" approach, and is reliant on human interaction and tacit knowledge transfer.

Knowledge transferred from the primary to the secondary affiliate may originate in the foreign parent or from other sources, such as from primary affiliate learning or from the local parent in an IJV. Secondary knowledge transfer is illustrated in Figure 1.

Figure 1. Secondary and Reverse Knowledge Transfer – Schematic Diagram

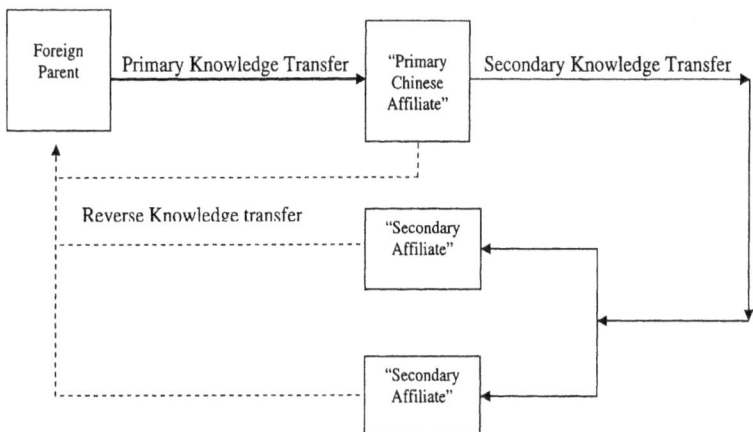

Reverse transfer is also shown in Figure 1. Local and foreign parents can become not only recipients but also agents for disseminating the knowledge of their own affiliates. This created knowledge might include context-specific management skills and social knowledge. These result from the localisation of western management skills combined with social knowledge gained in the local market. The possibility of affiliates' impact on parental learning clearly points to reverse knowledge transfer. Context-specific knowledge can be generated and re-applied in similar national or regional markets (Lyles/Salk 1996). This 'harvesting' of practices that have been created within the MNE may facilitate subsequent investments (Lyles 1988) and would be diagnostic of organisational learning (Lindholm 1998). Technological advances made by these affiliates can also be part of the package. The level and balance of the elements in reverse transfer will be indicative of the firm's strategy and of its success in execution. The strategy of the MNE will influence not only the type of knowledge that is dominant in primary knowledge transfer, but also that in reverse and secondary transfer. However, this has not been fully integrated into the literature on organisational learning within MNEs, and a number of questions remain. If the primary knowledge management strategy is based on re-use, then does it follow that any secondary transfer will be a carbon copy of the primary, or is it different? If it is based on knowledge creation, then will secondary transfer be similarly oriented? In the context of a re-use strategy, it is possible for reverse transfer to occur.

A few studies exist of reverse transfer concentrating on scientific (hard) technology between firms in developed countries, in circumstances where a knowledge creation strategy can be inferred (Frost 1998, Ghoshal/Bartlett 1988, Nohria/Ghoshal 1997, Yamin 1997, Håkanson/Nobel 2001). The most recent study by Håkanson and Nobel (2001) – of Swedish R & D WOSs – finds that the probability of reverse transfer increases with the level of organisational integration with the parent and the innovativeness of the affiliate. The weakly negative independent effect of local WOS embededdeness is an indication that local influences on knowledge management strategy are as yet not fully understood, and that theory is lacking. The dynamic structure of the relationship between knowledge transfer and learning is also unresolved. The view that knowledge transfer and organisational learning begin simultaneously with the establishment of a new affiliate (Inkpen 1995a, 1995b) does not sit easily with the premise that successful prior execution of primary transfer is a requirement for secondary transfer. The relationship between knowledge transfer and learning will be investigated in the case analysis.

Organisational Learning under Different Forms of Ownership

The choice of WOS versus IJV ownership is unlikely to be neutral with respect to knowledge transfer. It is true that both qualify as internalised forms of international business, and therefore should be expected to facilitate the transfer of the tacit component of technology (Hennart 1982), which is the hallmark of interactive learning. However, the IJV is also a collaborative mode, and therefore provides opportunities for mistrust and opportunism.

The existing IJV literature focuses on the conditions in which the JV is the optimal entry mode. It gives scant attention to the circumstances in which the JV form is a legal requirement, and in which the freedom to select the partner is limited or absent, as is often the case in an emerging host. The literature stresses the importance of selecting a partner that offers complementarity in capabilities, compatibility in management strategies, and low risk of becoming a competitor (Buckley/Glaister 2002, Porter/Fuller 1986). However, if few of the desirable qualities of an IJV partner are present, we should expect implications for knowledge transfer and organisational learning. Empirical studies by Beamish (1985) and Beamish and Banks (1987) of IJVs in developing countries point to the likelihood of excess transaction costs experienced by forced joint ventures with local firms or government bodies. The relevant theory of how this impacts on knowledge transfer and organisational learning is largely absent, and at present can only be extrapolated from studies of unconstrained IJVs between developed country partners.

Buckley and Casson (1988) argue that lack of trust between the partners and the absence of consensus over goals increase transaction costs in IJVs and thus diminish absorptive capacity. These barriers may be considerable, but they can change over time. There is a dynamic dimension to generating trust within an IJV. Trust may result from the growth of cooperation by "taking the easy decisions first" (Buckley/Glaister 2002, p. 62). However, the literature currently gives no guidance on whether this might be expected to extend to knowledge transfer. Taxonomically, learning can be of the "knowledge transfer type" (how to transfer knowledge), or of the "how to engage in a JV" variety. This can be specific to a particular JV, or generic so as to produce "joint venture sophisticated firms" (Lyles 1988). Joint venture sophistication on the part of parent firms would suggest that they should be predisposed towards JVs. But would this still apply if primary market entry were via a forced IJV?

The Model

The theoretical discussion suggests that ownership structure determines the strategy set. Two ownership modes have been followed in establishing FIEs in China; WOSs and JVs with local Chinese entities. We hypothesise three strategy sets: an "in-house" strategy for WOSs, a "constrained-strategy" for JVs with a sleeping partner, and a "joint" strategy for a JV with an active partner (contrast Cannice/Daniels (2000) where ownership "operating mode" *follows* international strategy, environment and technology transfer costs). "Sleeping partners" are usually government nominees who theoretically oversee operations in China and participate in decision making, but who are normally content with a distant, consultative role. "Active partners" are normally manufacturers of cognate products with pre-existing manufacturing facilities. The "active partners" constrain the foreign entrants into using their facilities, making this type of entry more like a takeover than a greenfield entry. This can be crucial because, unlike WOSs and JVs with sleeping partners, old vintage capital, technology and management will be brought into the JV by the Chinese partner. WOSs therefore are unconstrained by their ownership structure, but JVs may have pre-existing management and labour obligations to honour (particularly where they are denied the choice of JV partner), which require the continuing employment of an excessively large workforce and poor facilities to the cost of the FIE.

In practice, the line of demarcation between the two categories of JVs may not always be entirely clear. Further, our model may be interpreted as if the foreign entrant has full knowledge of the JV partner. This is often not the case – many instances of Chinese partners not making their true economic circumstances known to their prospective partners have occurred (Child 2000). The motivation of the Chinese JV partner is also likely to differ from that of the foreign entrant. "What seems to be missing from Chinese thinking, however, is any detailed bu-

Figure 2. The Model

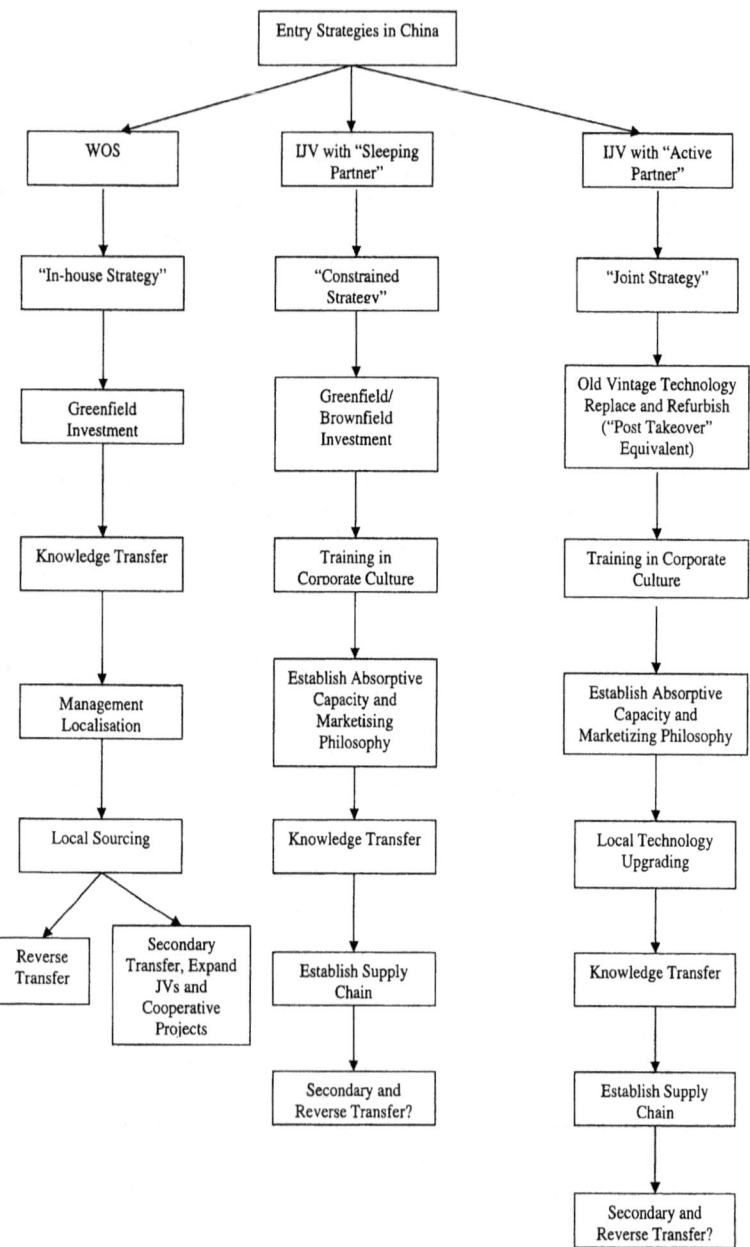

siness analysis at the corporate level of why either side is involved in the JVs" (Zhu/Speece/So 1998, p. 24). Modifying this thinking – introducing "marketized" attitudes – is difficult for many FIEs. One expatriate manager quoted by Rosen (1999, p. 50) on the imperative of avoiding goal conflict says "The JV still works in China, but if you do use it, do so with someone who is not in your industry – they are Neanderthals. Go with someone who just wants to make money...".

Figure 2 shows our preliminary model. The later stages of the model, concerning secondary and reverse transfer are the least complete, and require theoretical development. The strategies, as determined by the ownership structure and type of partner, play out in different ways. The WOS is free to invest, transfer knowledge and localise management, thus internalising the development of absorptive capacity (Buckley/Casson 1976). It can then establish local sourcing of inputs (a major difficulty in China – given the difficulties of procurement, and constraints on importing components), and establish its network in China. JVs are constrained by their partners. At best, the sleeping partner will have no "baggage" (dated old vintage capital, management outlook and facilities), at worst, this will be brownfield entry, akin to the takeover of a bundle of resources, most of which the foreign entrant will not want but which will impose a large, ongoing cost on the FIE in terms of scrap machinery and a huge under-employed, unskilled workforce (See Steinfeld (1998) for details of the difficulties in reforming state-owned enterprises in China). Establishing equilibrium here is likely to be costly and time consuming. It represents a major managerial headache for JVs in China. Only when this is corrected can absorptive capacity of all but the most rudimentary kind be established (see the recent references to conflicts in the IJVs of Peugeot Citroen and Pepsico in China (Financial Times 2002b and 2002c)). Our model suggests JVs will be much slower in achieving primary knowledge transfer than will WOSs. There will also be a need to retrain old style managers and inculcate a modern corporate culture into the JV. This is likely to divert managerial attention from the real task of establishing a presence in China and penetrating Chinese and global markets. Figure 2 is a schematic attempt to capture these divergent strategies. It suggests that the process of knowledge transfer to China is predetermined by the ownership mode of entry. Moreover it suggests that primary knowledge transfer – from the parent to the Chinese affiliate – will be swifter in WOSs than in JVs. Thus the age of the affiliate is a subordinate determinant of successful initial transfer and therefore of secondary and reverse transfer. Figure 2 expresses this in terms of the number of stages that have to be traversed before knowledge transfer can be effective.

The importance of affiliate age is emphasised by Håkanson and Nobel (2001) for Swedish MNEs, although it is not subordinated to ownership in the absolute fashion of our model. Håkanson and Nobel find that "embeddedness in the local network" is a positive factor in achieving knowledge (technology) transfer. Our model suggests that embeddedness in the local network may inhibit and delay successful primary transfer (and therefore subsequent reverse and secondary transfer). This arises from the need to spend time, effort and management resources on upgrading local partners and suppliers in terms of legacy factors (facilities, management and technology). Establishing absorptive capacity in the JV and introducing a marketising philosophy in state owned entities can seriously delay (even prevent) the introduction of knowledge.

However, after a (long) period of upgrading, learning and infusion of new resources, the connections with JV partners may produce contracts and protection unavailable to WOSs. The favouritism shown to those connected to the state may pay dividends in the longer run for JVs. We therefore suggest, in contrast to Håkanson and Nobel, that in China and comparable emerging economies a U-shaped relationship exists between "strong local embeddedness" and successful knowledge transfer. However, the upturn of the U may be considerably delayed unless favourable market conditions, declining costs and successful cooperation favour the JV. The positive relationship between local embeddedness and successful operation predicted by Håkanson and Nobel may be a distant dream for many JVs. In contrast, in the absence of government discrimination against them, WOSs will not carry this burden and are likely to effect successful knowledge transfer more rapidly than JVs. Our model utilises secondary and reverse transfer as diagnostic of the success of primary transfer. These are, to a large extent, codetermined by entry strategy in that wholly owned operation is a signal of full integration into the MNE's system. It should be borne in mind that Håkanson and Nobel examine only WOS (in R & D) and therefore cover only half of the range of potential ownership entry decisions.

Research Method

This paper is an exercise in theory building rather than the testing of theory, employing a multiple-case design (Yin 1994). The gaps and conflicts in the body of theory reviewed permit a preliminary model to be constructed using existing theoretical concepts. We chose a case study approach consisting of two firms because our research questions centre on the "how" and "why" of knowledge transfer in the emerging market of China. This procedure enables us to generate new theoretical concepts grounded in case and cross-case analysis (Herriott/Firestone 1983).

Data Collection

Most of the major telecommunications equipment manufacturers produce in the Chinese market (Wu 1995, Andersen Consulting 1997). Nineteen companies met the selection criterion of a minimum of five years' production experience in China (Inkpen 1995b, Lyles/Salk 1996). A positive response was received from seven firms. Two firms were eliminated because they lacked the resources to cooperate and were unable to provide access within the time schedule of the field research. Following pilot fieldwork, Shanghai Bell and Motorola (China) were selected, as both were large final assemblers. This meant that they had engaged in knowledge transfer to a greater extent than the three other firms, which were component suppliers only. These two firms topped the FDI league table of inward investors in China (MOFTEC 1996) and remain dominant players in China's telecommunications equipment market (Financial Times 2001 a and 2001 b). Their size ensured that we were able to interview multiple respondents within each firm, which is a distinctive advantage of this study.

The pilot phase involved collecting secondary data and obtaining sufficient information to make the final selection of case study firms. Data collection protocols (e.g., letters and a semi-structured questionnaire) were designed for use in the fieldwork. In Phase 2, two rounds of in-depth interviews were carried out. Mixtures of open-ended and semi-structured interviews were conducted within each firm. The interviewees were asked general questions first, then pre-determined and follow-up questions. Data from the twenty-four interviews with twenty-three interviewees were transcribed from tapes. Postal communications with the interviewees were maintained to ensure accuracy.

The interviewees were senior executives, including those responsible for functional divisions such as business planning, marketing, finance, production and human resources. Members of the knowledge transfer team, such as the training manager, operational manager, project engineer and other technical professionals, were also interviewed. As the interviewees consisted of both foreign expatriates and Chinese, the English version of the questionnaire was carefully translated into Chinese. Back translation, as suggested by Brislin (1970), was carried out to verify the content consistency between the two versions of the questionnaire.

Data Analysis

Interview data and field notes were analysed by using the 'critical incident' approach suggested by Erlandson et al. (1993), involving the recording of significant and meaningful data in descriptive terms, and structuring the data to focus on emerging themes. This was achieved through coding both secondary and primary data, according to the theoretical propositions and issues identified in previous research. For example, all the interview transcripts were coded by both "content" (such as "technology transfer" and "personnel exchanges") and "importance" ("very important", "important", "relevant" and "irrelevant") paragraph by paragraph. Irrelevant materials were removed to reduce data (Miles/Huberman, 1984) and to highlight "theoretical properties and categories" (Glaser/Strauss 1967).

Using a "within-case" analysis, theory was first developed by examining the context of knowledge transfer in one case. Then, pattern matching (Miles/Huberman 1984, Yin 1994) was adopted to compare the finding from this first case with the second. Commonalties and differences of knowledge transfer practices between them were identified and reasons responsible were established with gained data and through prolonged contacts with interviewees. While the focus of investigation in the first case was "what" and "how", in the second this shifted to "why" there were differences between the cases and the theoretical impact arising from them for our preliminary model. Our findings and conclusions are generated from this process of raw data analysis combined with juxtaposition with the model, and are in the form of revised and new theoretical propositions. Wherever possible, the interview data was checked by triangulation with a second and independent source.

Profiles of the Two Firms

Motorola set up its representative office in Beijing in 1987. In 1992, it established Motorola (China) Electronics Ltd (Motorola (China)) in Tianjin, producing pagers, cellular phones, two-way radios, network equipment, semiconductor, auto electronics and accessories, largely for sale in China and other Asian markets. In following its four-point business strategy (investment and technology transfer; management localisation; local sourcing; JVs and cooperative projects), Motorola (China) has made US$3.4 billion investment in China. By 2000, Motorola (China) had established one wholly-owned company and seven JVs. It is now the largest foreign investor in China's telecommunications manufacturing sector.

Shanghai Bell Telephone Equipment Manufacturing Company Ltd (Shanghai Bell) was established in 1983 as a JV between Belgian Bell (32 per cent of equity), the Belgian government (8 per cent) and China's Postal and Telecommunications Industries Corporation (PTIC), part of the former Ministry of Post and Telecommunications (MPT, now Ministry of Information Industry) (60 per cent). In 1986, Alcatel acquired Belgian Bell, becoming Alcatel Bell. However, Shanghai Bell still reports to Alcatel Bell in Antwerp, Belgium. It specialises in the production and installation of Alcatel 1000 S1240 exchanges and related parts and components. By 2000 Shanghai Bell had 12 subsidiaries in China and two in Europe.

Findings

Entry Strategy, Ownership Form and Partner Selection

By the time Motorola entered the Chinese market the law on inward investment permitted the WOS form, which it chose in preference to an IJV. Motorola's affiliate was named Motorola (China), and its first activity was the greenfield establishment in Tianjin of two wholly-owned factories (1992 and 1994). The affiliate serviced a fast growing and highly competitive local consumer market, with 10–20 per cent of production for export. As a WOS, Motorola (China) enjoyed total discretion over recruitment and the sourcing of inputs. Changes in the law on foreign ownership meant that Motorola could begin with a WOS but these changes did not apply retrospectively, thus locking Alcatel Bell into its IJV structure. Shanghai Bell's primary business area was fixed line telephony equipment. The firm became a dominant supplier of digital exchanges that replaced the ageing analogue infrastructure. This strategy could be guaranteed by Alcatel Bell's IJV partner (PTIC), the industrial arm of the then MPT, and the local post and telecommunications bureaux (PTBs).

Primary Knowledge Transfer Strategy

Everything on Motorola's primary Tianjin site, from production equipment to organisational structure, from architectural design to corporate culture, was brought in simultaneously from Motorola in the USA or from subsidiaries elsewhere in the worldwide group. A wide range of knowledge was transferred with which the affiliate constructed the Semiconductor Plant, the Back End Plant, the Pager Plant, the Cellular Phone Plant, the Component and Power Source Parts Plant, and the Semiconductor Wafer Fabrication Plant. A benefit of the main output of the affiliate, mobile handsets, is that they are fully interoperable with the new mobile networks in China, constructed to the GSM standard, and required little adaptation.

Since the foundation of the affiliate, Motorola (China) has used extensive short term staff movements internationally in order to personalise knowledge. Expatriates were used on short term assignments, declining from over 30 per cent of management positions to less than 15 per cent. The affiliate selected for English language ability in its recruitment. It also invested heavily in the language training of its Chinese employees, to ensure that all were able to use the working language of Motorola. This achieved organisational integration, both within the affiliate and between the affiliate and the group. This created a multinational learning network based on human interaction independent of the structure of the group, rich in tacit knowledge transfer.

Alcatel Bell's primary affiliate was limited to the production of just one product – its public digital switching system, System 1240, for the Chinese market. All the production technologies transferred to Shanghai Bell concerned this product (customised large scale integration production, thick film hybrids, double sided and multilayer printed circuit boards, fully automated assembly line/surface mounting technology, computerised test facilities, and numerically controlled equipment for piece part manufacturing). Significantly, the firm quantified the transfer in codified form (technical documents and protocols covering more than 1,000 items of different specifications in fifteen categories relating to production and testing, plus related computer software and state-of-the-art equipment). In marked contrast to mobile telephony, product adaptation (both anticipated and unanticipated) was necessary for this equipment to connect with the ageing Chinese infrastructure.

Unlike Motorola, primary technologies were not transferred simultaneously, but rather in a series of stages in a "from easy to difficult" approach. The first related to assembling and testing of complete components imported from the foreign parent. Underlying this gradualism were obstacles to relocating the technologies to the affiliate. The JV contract provided only for product and production related technologies and the target dates for their transfer. No provision was made in the contract for the transfer of management and other soft skills, and recognition of the importance of social knowledge was entirely missing. This inhibited interaction as a means of knowledge transfer and imparts a bias away from soft skills. To some extent this can be laid at the door of the Chinese partner's emphasis on hard technologies. But by the time of the data collection (1997–1998) Shanghai Bell still employed 15 Belgian expatriates on long term contract. This, combined with the shortfall in localisation, suggests the proposition that a forced JV is more likely to suffer from goal conflict and absorptive capacity constraints than either an unfettered JV or a WOS. Furthermore, we propose that the foreign parent in a forced IJV will seek to maintain control through expatriate managers.

The deficit in the transfer of essential skills became apparent in the IJV, and this gap was later addressed by informal transfers outside the contract through the training and exchange of personnel, extending the timescale of primary knowledge transfer. At the conclusion of this process, Alcatel Bell's expertise in operation and management had been conveyed to the IJV, in the form of articulable technical and management knowledge, again congruent with the codification strategy identified in the earlier transfer. This included corporate governance and organisational models, systems for human resources management and production management, together with financial practices, marketing expertise and quality control systems[2].

The low absorptive capacity of Shanghai Bell stemmed from a lack of consensus over the goals of the firm. The wishes of the foreign parent to create a research-based affiliate as part of a learning network came to nothing. The Chinese partner resisted the transplant of the foreign parent's research strategy[3]. The IJV enjoyed an assured market because of central and local government procurement policies. One senior Belgian manager explained the preference of the Chinese partner for the IJV as a replicator of existing products:

"The reason for this is that the market situation is so wonderful that the Chinese side just don't listen to you. We have no choice. [. . .] When production is six million lines a year and the JV's major shareholder and biggest customer is MPT, why should they worry about the next generation products? They try to extend the life cycle of the present products, which is wrong. In a one billion people market, it is not difficult to find customers." (Senior manager, Alcatel Bell)

This dominant market position provided little incentive to the Chinese partner for the IJV to innovate. This only intensified when events in Tiananmen Square resulted in an embargo on equipment supply to China, leaving the domestic market for local producers alone.

From the timing of the adoption of a codified primary transfer strategy, it appears that it was a coping response to the low absorptive capacity of the affiliate. A documentation and language translation centre was instituted in 1985, after the establishment of Shanghai Bell, in order to progress the transfer of technology which was failing to meet targets. The language issue, which was addressed by universal training in Motorola (China), was in Shanghai Bell addressed by the creation of a translation group, to convert materials from the parent into Chinese, for distribution to the relevant departments. This, therefore, absolved much of the workforce from mastering technical material in a foreign language. This codification strategy militated against organisational integration both within the IJV (across the language barrier) and between the IJV and the foreign parent. The scope to create a learning network was limited to the training and international placements that did occur for certain Chinese staff in the Belgian headquarters.

The division of labour in the IJV displays asymmetry between the partners with key posts retained by the foreign partner. The Chinese partner made a significant input into human resources. However, this input was often negative. Promotions desired by the foreign partner of Chinese employees were blocked if they were not accepted by the Communist Party branch inside the IJV.

On the basis of this analysis, we propose that it is not the lack of complementarities between the partners that appears the most damaging to knowledge transfer to the IJV (and ultimately to organisational learning in the MNE). Rather, it is goal conflicts. The failure in terms of under and mis-investment in R & D and human resources creates shortcomings in absorptive capacity. The IJV then faces a discrete choice in favour of a re-use strategy to avoid escalation in the cost of knowledge transfer (Hansen/Nohria/Tierney 1999). Thus interactive learning, rich in tacit knowledge, is suppressed and knowledge creation is eschewed. Our cross-case analysis suggests the proposition that when an IJV is formed under legal obligation, it is more likely to adopt a coping strategy of knowledge re-use even though its foreign parent might employ a creation strategy.

The "from easy to difficult" transfer to Shanghai Bell also has resonance with the building of trust between the partners of an IJV, in respect of "taking the easy decisions first". In circumstances where the transfer of technology is problematic, the transfer of knowledge objects in a documentation centre was likely to satisfy the appetite of the Chinese partner for hard technology. This practice encapsulates the shift in affiliate strategy away from the creation of new technology. This suggests the proposition that, where the goals of the partners diverge, the original business and knowledge management strategy of the IJV may be sacrificed in order to accommodate the local partner's preference. This may reduce tensions and conflict, but it exacerbates structural dissimilarity with the foreign parent in knowledge processing making subsequent transfer more costly. Therefore, in line with our preliminary model, we propose that for a forced IJV (for which the likelihood of goal mismatch is heightened) conflicts will ensue. These, requiring resolution, will lengthen the stages in knowledge transfer, and add to their number. As a survival strategy, the goals of the IJV will be downgraded to limit these costs.

The implication for our model is that business and knowledge management strategy will follow structure when ownership structure is imposed. The remaining question is: how can primary knowledge transfer be linked theoretically to secondary and reverse transfer?

Secondary Transfer

Since March 1995, Motorola (China) has formed seven JVs with local partners in China, to which the two wholly-owned factories have made secondary transfers. These JVs were created to manufacture a range of high-technology products, from pagers and multi-media computers to CDMA (Code Division Multiple Access) infrastructure and semiconductor products. These JVs were intended to collaborate in R & D with Motorola (China), and to generate new products, rather than merely reproducing Motorola products. Each of Motorola (China)'s JV partners were state-owned industrial concerns (as opposed to being government bodies), with their own records of technology creation and development. The choice of lo-

Figure 3. Secondary Knowledge Transfer by Motorola (China)

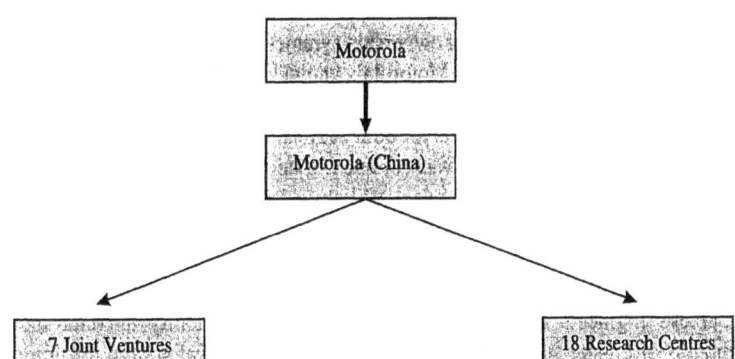

Keys:

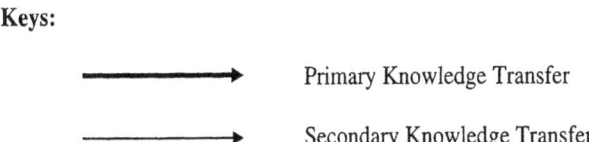
                               Primary Knowledge Transfer

                               Secondary Knowledge Transfer

cal industrial partners created a local production base and a positive image with local authorities. These JVs were intended to enable Motorola to achieve a technological, as well as a production, division of labour within China and to gain scale economies (Figure 3). JV establishment was also considered essential to gain access to individual provincial markets.

Motorola (China) secondary affiliates' operations represent a subset of the activities of the primary affiliate, and the secondary transfer itself is therefore delimited. In contrast with its primary knowledge practice, Motorola (China) contractually assigned "expatriates" to the secondary affiliates. These were Chinese, not foreigners. Motorola had six JV affiliates in China with a variety of regional partners. These secondary affiliates were the only manufacturers of multi-system cellular phones in China, and their products were sold in the USA and Europe.

Motorola (China) transferred multiple application technology, system integration, security technology, and design and manufacturing expertise to the secondary affiliates. This was characteristically less sophisticated than that in the primary transfer, but it did include technology generated in the primary affiliate, such as the facial design of mobile phones (including new functional keys) and Chinese software. Local governments heavily regulated local markets, and a key factor in selecting JVs for the secondary affiliates was the marketing ability of the Chinese partners, especially their influence on local government procurement. The affiliates also became after-sales service centres for the group's products.

Despite the lesser degree of ownership symmetry between the primary and secondary affiliates (being JVs) Motorola's knowledge management strategy took the form of a learning network. The strategy of secondary technology transfer remained to manufacture products for both national and international markets. The level of management training was commensurate with this product development function. Accordingly, the secondary affiliates adopted Motorola's organisational structure, financial and human resources management practices, and quality control systems. This training includes direct inputs from Motorola worldwide (e.g, before the Leshan-Phoenix Semiconductor Company Ltd started production, key Chinese engineers travelled to Motorola's Seremban facility in Malaysia for months of on-site specialised training). The quality control system of Motorola (China)'s JVs also equated both to the primary affiliate and the parent worldwide. For example, Motorola (China) established Smartcard System Co., Ltd. and Beijing Huamin Smartcard System Manufacturing Co., Ltd. in June 1998 and has brought to the JVs Motorola's Six-Sigma quality system in services and products to provide "total customer satisfaction".

A crucial aspect of secondary transfer is the local sourcing of inputs, as this requires the transfer of technologies and skills to produce key components. A government policy of tax and tariff penalties applied to FIE localisation rates of under eighty per cent. This effected a pressure to create a network of local suppliers. In the face of general scarcity of quality component suppliers with adequate absorptive capacity, Motorola (China)'s approach was to manufacture a number of components in-house (as in our model), and simultaneously establish a number of research centres with local partners and potential suppliers to develop new products. This strategy raises local embeddedness and is congruent with internal organisational integration of the MNE.

Shanghai Bell's secondary affiliates were also JVs, but with local government bodies, such as local bureaux, rather than industrial partners. This replicated the partnering strategy of Shanghai Bell on a smaller scale. Such partners helped the affiliates to circumvent local market access barriers. Local government representatives on the boards of the secondary affiliates played no role in operational matters. For example, in Northeast Asia Telecommunications Manufacturing Co. (NEAT) the management team was under a board of directors drawn from Shanghai Bell and from two Provincial Bureaux of Liaoning Province. Although Shanghai Bell was a minority shareholder, it played the dominant role.

As with Motorola, Shanghai Bell's transfers to its secondary affiliates were a subset in both scale and scope of those originally transferred to the primary affiliate, to create a division of labour. Activities were displaced as the core competence originally transferred from the foreign parent was relocated in secondary affiliates, e.g., coils and miniature transformers to NEAT, but without the inclu-

Figure 4. Secondary and Reverse Knowledge Transfer in Shanghai Bell

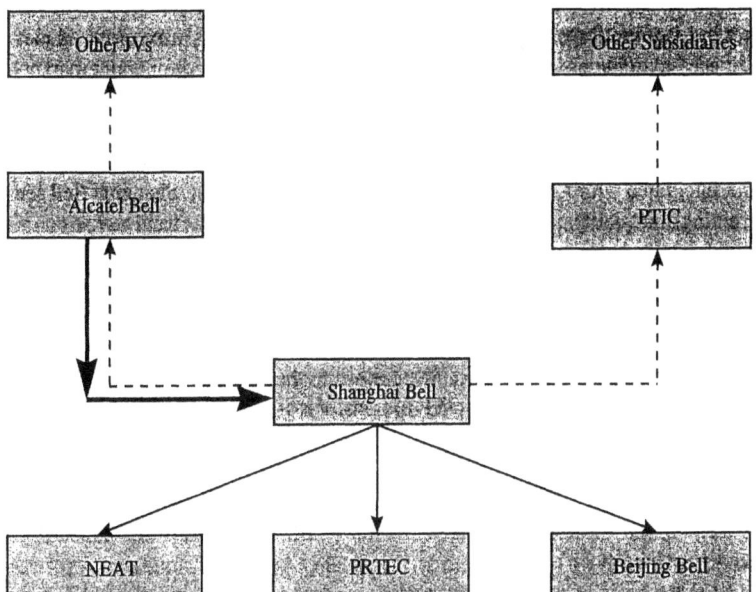

Keys:

    ⟶   Primary Knowledge Transfer

    ⟶   Secondary Knowledge Transfer

    --------⟶   Reverse Knowledge Transfer

sion of technology generated in the primary affiliate (as was the case with Motorola (China). In common with Motorola (China), secondary affiliates performed a crucial after sales service and marketing role. Figure 4 illustrates the transfer of technologies, management skills and social knowledge by Shanghai Bell to three of its affiliates.

Of the three affiliates of Shanghai Bell, two were engaged in the manufacture of parts and the assembly of the final product using parts from Shanghai Bell, including some parts imported from Alcatel Bell. NEAT produced non-power inductor coils, miniature transformers, and the processing, sale, installation, testing and after sales service of the S1240 series and other telecommunications equipment. NEAT was distinctive in that it was established to service a large market in Liaoning Province, where Shanghai Bell had previously experienced market access problems. The other two affiliates were established for wider markets.

Human resources management practices demonstrate the contrast in knowledge management strategies. The managers of the secondary affiliates attended Shanghai Bell's training centre annually, but unlike Motorola's policy, this was not integrated within the training system of the foreign parent. Shanghai Bell sent training and quality assurance officers to its affiliates to inspect and advise on improvements. As with Motorola (China), Shanghai Bell assigned "expatriates" to key positions in the secondary affiliates, and these were often Chinese. Executives from Shanghai Bell occupied the general manager's position of NEAT and the managerships of the finance and engineering departments. Thus a similar stock of expertise and knowledge percolated down to the affiliates, in an extension of the primary transfer. The JV 'model' of transfer was re-applied to Shanghai Bell's affiliates, including the "from easy to difficult" approach. The secondary affiliates were only involved in manufacturing and assembly for local markets so mirroring, on a smaller scale, the approach of Shanghai Bell. This suggests the wholesale transfer of the knowledge management strategy of the primary affiliate, under the same constraints.

On the basis of our case comparison, we propose that if the ownership form of the primary affiliate is an IJV formed under legal requirement, then the secondary affiliates will also tend to be JVs. This form better suits the re-use knowledge management strategy of the IJV, and therefore the secondary transfer of knowledge between donor and recipient. In contrast, a primary WOS remains free to choose the optimal organisational form and, if relevant, Chinese partners for its secondary affiliates. The imperative of local market access in regulated markets militates in favour of the secondary JV form even when the primary affiliate is a WOS.

In respect of local embeddedness, the response of Shanghai Bell to the pressures to localise took a different path to that at Motorola (China). While knowledge transfer to the secondary affiliates localised the production of basic components, there was no local network of research and development partnerships to outsource production. Outsourcing was of the most basic items to suppliers with links to the IJV and JV partners.

Thus, we theorise that embeddedness may be of two types. The first comprises linkages that are created by the MNE specifically to construct a local loop in its international learning network. Organisational integration and local embeddedness of type one are linked to a common factor – a knowledge creation strategy. The second type of embeddedness consists of inherited linkages under obligation to a local JV partner. Our model suggests that the second embeddedness in the local network may well be a factor that inhibits and delays successful primary transfer (and therefore subsequent reverse and secondary transfer) but which may, after a considerable delay, confer benefits on the affiliate. In contrast, WOSs with the first type of embeddedness are likely to effect successful knowledge transfer more rapidly than JVs (the direct relationship identified by Håkanson and Nobel (2001)).

Reverse Transfer

From the outset it was intended that Motorola (China) should conduct research and development to create new products for the multinational group, in a globally linked innovation system. This results from Motorola's global strategy to develop local technological capacity, rather than achieve market access through IJV partnering. The affiliate's new product development served the needs of the whole multinational. The flow of technology-related resources and outputs from the affiliate to other units of Motorola was the result of a planned division of labour within the multinational group. Regional product mandates were allocated to Motorola (China) with its associated R & D design centres. This integration was repeated in a number of fields, e.g., software development, where research in China made an input into worldwide product development. This created the capacity to remit knowledge (largely technical) to other parts of the Motorola group.

A number of expatriate managers and engineers sent to China were ethnic Chinese, headed by a Chinese American with twenty years' experience of doing business in the region. Subsequently, knowledge acquired locally was employed by Motorola (China) to re-invest in the Chinese market. Organisational integration was witnessed in the transfer of selected Chinese managers to the USA, to improve headquarters-subsidiary coordination. This personnel movement within Motorola indicates informal reverse knowledge transfer about Chinese business culture, i.e., a learning network not discernible from the MNE's formal structure.

Although Alcatel Bell was a research-intensive multinational, there had been very little R & D in Shanghai Bell for the reasons presented earlier. The knowledge transferred from Shanghai Bell to Alcatel Bell was confined to local management skills and social knowledge accumulated from ten years' operation in Shanghai Bell. It was employed by Alcatel Bell in its subsequent investments in China.

The western parent chose a different line of business for its six directly owned Chinese JV affiliates (as distinct from the secondary affiliates of Shanghai Bell), so that these investments would not pose any threat to Shanghai Bell, and therefore to the relationship with the Chinese partner. An Alcatel Bell manager explained:

"We have another six joint ventures in the Chinese market, but not in the same product markets [switching systems] as Shanghai Bell. These joint ventures are producing some "smaller" products, such as connectors, mobile phones.

They are all relatively successful. Certainly the market growth has helped a lot. But the experience of managing Shanghai Bell really enabled us on how to proceed with joint ventures in the Chinese market." (Senior manager, Alcatel Bell)

Knowledge transferred to Alcatel Bell concerned practices and experience in dealing with JV partners, and in extracting knowledge from these partners about how best to configure business within China (including local suppliers, central and local governments, and other stakeholders such as banks, consumer groups):

"Having experienced various problems in Shanghai Bell when we first entered the Chinese market, we changed the way of doing business in the subsequent subsidiaries we established by integrating our lessons learned in the design and process of operations of these firms. Indeed, we are seeking more input from the Chinese side in decision making." (Senior manager, Alcatel Bell)

This response suggests that the parent firm had learned non-partner-specific knowledge about joint venturing in China, and in particular about the type of joint venture partner needed. The later joint venture partners of Alcatel Bell were all industrial partners, similar to those chosen by Motorola (China). As with Motorola, tacit knowledge was acquired by the western parent on understanding the host culture, the mentality of local employees, and the custom of doing business in the local market.

Figure 4 presents a comprehensive picture of the knowledge transfer in Shanghai Bell, including primary knowledge transfer from Alcatel Bell to Shanghai Bell, indicated by the thick line starting the knowledge transfer process. The knowledge transfer from Shanghai Bell to its own affiliates, indicated in the thin lines, is part of the secondary knowledge transfer. The remaining part of the process is reverse knowledge transfer from Shanghai Bell to both parents. In the case of the Chinese parent, PTIC, this reverse transfer is limited to the management training received by staff supplied to the JV, who subsequently rejoin the parent. It is now common for the western parent in Sino-foreign JVs to place a restriction in the JV contract that staff supplied to the JV should not return to the Chinese parent within a stipulated period. This is to limit the expense of JV training that brings little benefit to the JV. However, little can be done to prevent staff leaving the JV to join rival firms, other than to improve the retention of staff through remuneration and career opportunities. As Shanghai Bell was such an early entrant into the Chinese market, it did become an 'academy for the industry', experiencing considerable loss of staff to both Chinese and foreign-owned competitors.

The contrasting experiences of the two affiliates in reverse transfer result from differences in strategy arising from ownership structure as outlined in the model, and drawing on the economics of supplying regional or global markets. In Shanghai Bell, the Chinese partner and the JV structure have locked the firm into serving the Chinese market alone employing a knowledge re-use strategy. Our analysis suggests the proposition that, when a knowledge re-use strategy is in force, the nature of reverse knowledge transfer will be predominantly implicit and related to local operational conditions. The implicit knowledge remitted will not be governed by a formal contract. Under a re-use model, knowledge flow is primarily towards the market, not in reverse.

From a comparison of our cases we propose that the balance of tacit versus explicit knowledge in reverse transfer differs with the knowledge management strategy of the MNE in the host. Reverse transfers of tacit local knowledge occur under both strategies, not governed by a formal contract. However, a knowledge creation strategy in the affiliate implies the formal remission of explicit knowledge, accompanied by tacit knowledge linked to the technology.

The process through which reverse knowledge transfer results in learning at the MNE level depends on the knowledge management strategy of the MNE in the host. This influences the composition and volume of transfer. Under a knowledge creation strategy, the affiliate is contractually obliged to generate and remit new knowledge, and the absorptive capacity of the MNE is already in place to receive formal reverse transfer. But under both strategies, reverse transfer of tacit local knowledge will be received where it can be employed in furthering the MNE's business strategy in the host. We propose, therefore, that MNE learning from reverse transfer of different classes of knowledge depends on formal knowledge management strategy, and on the MNE's wider business strategy in the host (or analogous) market, whether this is governed by a contract or not. A knowledge creation strategy will result in more explicit reverse transfers (with tacit knowledge linked to the technology) than a re-use one.

The cases suggest the proposition that knowledge transfer and organisational learning begin simultaneously with the establishment of a new affiliate. However, this is not the same as organisational learning at the level of the MNE. The unit of analysis must be specified. We therefore propose that, at the MNE level, both secondary and reverse transfer will succeed learning in the affiliate.

Conclusions

This paper has extended the theory of knowledge transfer and learning within multinational firms in an emerging economy. It is a theory-building study grounded in the context of the entry and operations of foreign multinational enterprises in Chinese manufacturing industry. Our primary results support the proposition that knowledge transfer is predetermined by entry strategy. Ownership structure on entry may lock foreign firms into constraints from which it is difficult to escape, causing a divergence from global business and knowledge management strategies. Our research also indicates that secondary and reverse knowledge transfer is conditional on the characteristics and success of primary transfer. Our findings highlight the crucial importance of local factors such as the congruence of goals, and the aptitude and ability of joint venture partners.

Our research suggests that local embeddedness may be of two types, both of which are determined by the nature of the knowledge management strategy in the primary affiliate. A knowledge creation strategy appears connected to international organisational integration and to a locally embedded learning network, extended through secondary transfer. Local embeddedness in the context of a forced re-use knowledge management strategy may be inimical to the rapid transfer of technology. Our propositions also suggest that reverse transfer differs in character between cases. Only a knowledge creation strategy promotes formal technology (with linked tacit knowledge) reverse transfer. However, the reverse transfer of tacit local knowledge appears to be a common factor independent of strategy.

Our study has considered the polar cases of constrained versus free ownership on entry. The applicability of our propositions should be tested on a continuum of entry conditions. While many industries in China have been liberalised, others will remain under some form of ownership restrictions during the programme of WTO liberalisation, e.g., telecommunications services. The Chinese government puts great emphasis on the inward transfer of the latest technology, and on the building of domestic technological capacity. The propositions put forward in this paper suggest that political control over sensitive industries may create impediments to these objectives that are underestimated. Research is also required on sectors in which a global re-use knowledge management strategy is freely chosen. Lastly, our propositions should be investigated in other restricted sectors, such as financial services which, although not technologically based, face similar challenges of global versus local strategic choice in knowledge management.

Endnotes

1 The authors are grateful for the comments of three anonymous referees and the Editor of the Special Issue. Financial support from the Universities' China Committee in London (UCCL) for conducting interviews in China is gratefully acknowledged.
2 A listing of the transferred technologies (hardware and software) initially appeared in a company publication (Alcatel Bell 1998). No reference was made to managerial knowledge transfer. The interviewed managers in Shanghai Bell and, with regard to secondary transfer, its subsidiary NEAT were all asked to confirm the transferred knowledge. It transpired from their answers that managerial knowledge had indeed been transferred. This was subsequently validated by managers at the headquarters of Alcatel Bell in Antwerp, Belgium.
3 The responses to the question on R & D were triangulated, and disagreement was found between the foreign parent and the Chinese interviewees in Shanghai Bell. Chinese respondents claimed that progress had been made in R & D, but this was contradicted by the testimony of the Belgian executives and managers. We interpret this as a difference in understanding about what constitutes R & D. The Belgians construed it conventionally as new technology creation, but the Chinese included the adaptation of existing products (necessary for the Chinese market).

References

Alcatel Bell, *Report on the Cooperation between Belgium and the People's Republic of China in the Field of Telecommunications,* Antwerp, Belgium 1998.
Andersen Consulting, *Inside the Chinese Automotive Industry: The Third Lean Enterprise Report,* London: Andersen Consulting 1997.
Beamish, P. W., The Characteristics of Joint Ventures in Developed and Developing Countries, *Columbia Journal of World Business,* 20, 3, 1985, pp. 13–19.
Beamish, P. W./Banks, J. C., Equity Joint Ventures and the Theory of Multinational Enterprise, *Journal of International Business Studies,* 17, 2, 1987, pp. 1–16.
Brislin, R., Back-Translation for Cross-Cultural Research, *Journal of Cross-Cultural Psychology,* 75, 1970, pp. 3–9.
Buckley, P. J./Casson, M., *The Future of the Multinational Enterprise,* London: Macmillan 1976.
Buckley, P. J./Casson, M., A Theory of Cooperation in International Business, in Contractor, F. J./Lorange, P. (eds), *Cooperative Strategies in International Business,* Lexington, MA: Lexington Books D C Heath & Co 1988.
Buckley, P. J./Glaister, K., What Do We Know about International Joint Ventures?, in Contractor, F./Lorange, P. (eds) *Cooperative Strategies and Alliances,* Oxford: Elsevier Science 2002.
Cannice, N./Daniels, J. D., Operating Modes and Performance: US High-Technology Ventures in China, in Li, J. T./Tsui, A. S./Weldon, E. (eds), *Management and Organizations in the Chinese Context,* London: Macmillan 2000, pp. 157–184.
Chang, S. J./Rosenzweig, P. M., A Process Model of MNC Evolution: The Case of Sony Corporation in the United States, *Carnegie Bosch Institute Working Paper 95–9,* Carnegie Mellon University 1995.
Child, J., Management and Organizations in China: Key Trends and Issues, in Li, J. T./Tsui, A. S./Weldon, E. (eds), *Management and Organizations in the Chinese Context,* London: Macmillan 2000, pp. 33–62.
Cohen, W. M./Levinthal, D. A., Absorptive Capacity: A New Perspective on Learning and Innovation, *Administrative Science Quarterly,* 35, 1990, pp.128–152.
Davenport, T. H./De Long, D. W./Beers, M. C., Successful Knowledge Management Projects, *Sloan Management Review,* Winter 1998, pp. 43–57.

Easterby-Smith, M./Crossan, M./Nicolini, D., Organizational Learning: Debates Past, Present and Future, *Journal of Management Studies*, 37, 6, 2000, pp. 783–796.
Engardio, P./Roberts, D./Symonds, W. C., Huge Market, Huge Headache, *Business Week*, 15th April, 1996, pp. 20–21.
Erlandson, D. A./Harris, L./Skipper, B. L./Allen, S. D., *Doing Naturalistic Inquiry: A Guide to Methods*, London: Sage 1993.
Financial Times, "Global Manufacturers Aim to Make It Big in China", p. 28, 24th October 2001a.
Financial Times, "Manufacturers Turn to China's Mobile Market", p. 25, 13th December 2001a.
Financial Times, "Telecoms Giant Splits into Two", p. 33, 17th May 2002a.
Financial Times, "Peugeot Seeks Shake-up of China Parts Sector", p. 31, 1st October 2002b.
Financial Times, "Bad Blood in Beverage Land", p. 18, 2nd October 2002c.
Frost, A. S., The Geographic Sources of Innovation in the Multinational Enterprise: US Subsidiaries and Host Country Spillovers, 1980–1990, Doctoral dissertation, Massachusetts Institute of Technology 1998.
Ghoshal, S./Bartlett, C. A., Creation, Adoption and Diffusion of Innovations by Subsidiaries of Multinational Companies, *Journal of International Business Studies*, 19, 1988, pp. 365–388.
Glaser, B. G./Strauss, A. L., *The Discovery of Grounded Theory: Strategies for Qualitative Research*, London: Weidenfeld and Nicolson 1967.
Håkanson, L./Nobel, R., Organizational Characteristics and Reverse Technology Transfer, *Management International Review*, 41, 4, 2001, pp. 395–420.
Hansen, M. T./Nohria, N./Tierney, T., What's Your Strategy for Managing Knowledge?, *Harvard Business Review*, March-April 1999, pp. 106–116.
Hedlund, G., The Hypermodern MNC – A Heterarchy?, *Human Resources Management*, 25, 1986, pp. 9–25.
Hedlund, G./Nonaka, J., Models of Knowledge Management in the West and Japan, in Lorange, P./Chakravarthy, B./Roos, J./Van de Ven, A. (eds), *Implementing Strategic Process: Change, Learning and Cooperation*, London: Basil Blackwell 1993, pp. 117–144.
Hennart, J. F., *A Theory of Multinational Enterprise*, Ann Arbour, MI: University of Michigan Press 1982.
Herriott, R. E./Firestone, W. A., Multisite Qualitative Policy Research: Optimising Description and Generalisability, *Educational Researcher*, 12, 1983, pp. 14–19.
Hymer, S. H., *The International Operations of National Firms: A Study of Direct Foreign Investment*, Cambridge, MA.: MIT Press (original thesis produced in 1960) 1976.
Inkpen, A. C., The Management of Knowledge in International Alliances, *Carnegie Bosch Institute Working Paper*, No. 95-1, 1995a.
Inkpen, A. C., *The Management of International Joint Ventures: An Organisational Learning Perspective*, London: Sage 1995b.
Kindleberger, C. P., *American Business Abroad*, New Haven: Yale University Press 1969.
Lane, P. J./Lubatkin, M., Relative Absorptive Capacity and Interorganizational Learning, *Strategic Management Journal*, 19, 1998, pp. 461–477.
Lemoine, L., FDI and the Opening Up of China's Economy, Centre D'Etedes Prospectives et D'Informaiton Internationales (CEPII), Working paper No. 00–11, June 2000.
Lindholm, N., Learning Modes in International Joint Ventures in China, in Selmer, J. (ed), *International Management in China: Cross-Cultural Issues*, London: Routledge 1998, pp. 45–56.
Luo, Y., *Multinational Corporations in China: Benefiting from Structural Transformation*, Copenhagen: Copenhagen Business School Press 2000.
Lyles, M. A., Learning Among Joint Venture Sophisticated Firms, *Management International Review*, 28, 1988, pp. 85–98.
Lyles, M. A./Salk, J. E., Knowledge Acquisition From Foreign Parents in International Joint Ventures: An Empirical Examination in the Hungarian Context, *Journal of International Business Studies*, 27, 5, 1996, pp. 877–903.
Magee, S. P., Information and the Multinational Corporations: An Appropriability Theory of Direct Foreign Investment, in Bhagwati, J. N. (ed), *The New International Economic Order: The North-South Debate*, Cambridge, Mass.: MIT Press 1977a, pp. 317–340.
Magee, S. P., Multinational Corporations, the Industry Technology Cycle and Development, *Journal of World Trade Law*, 2, 4, 1977b, pp. 297–321.

Miles, M. B./Huberman, A. M., *Qualitative Data Analysis: A Sourcebook of New Methods*, London: Sage 1984.
MOFTEC, *China's Top 500 Foreign-Funded Enterprises (1995–1996)*, Ministry Report, Beijing 1996.
Motorola in China, *Motorola (China) Internal Document*, Beijing: Motorola (China) 2000.
Nelson, R. R./Winter, S. G., *An Evolutionary Theory of Economic Change*, Cambridge, MA.: Harvard University Press 1982.
Nohria, N./Ghoshal, S., *The Differentiated Network – Organizing Multinational Corporations for Value Creation*, San Francisco, CA: Jossey-Bass 1997.
Pearce, R. D., *The Internationalization of Research and Development by Multinational Enterprises*, London: Macmillan 1989.
Porter, M. E./Fuller, M. B., Coalitions and Global Strategy, in Porter, M. E. (ed), *Competition in Global Industries*, Boston, MA: Harvard Business School Press 1986.
Roehrig, M. F., *Foreign Joint Ventures in Contemporary China*, New York: St. Martin's Press 1994.
Rosen, D. H., *Behind the Open Door: Foreign Enterprises in the Chinese Marketplace*, Washington DC: Institute for International Economics 1999.
Ruggles, R., The State of the Notion: Knowledge Management in Practice, *California Management Review*, 40, 3, 1998, pp. 80–89.
Steinfeld, E. S., *Forging Reform in China: The Fate of State-Owned Industry*, Cambridge: Cambridge University Press 1998.
Studwell, J., *The China Dream*, London: Profile Books 2002.
Tempest, S., Ideas Work: A Study of Learning in Network Contexts: The Case of the UK Television Industry, Ph.D thesis, University of Nottingham 1999.
Vernon, R., International Investment and International Trade in the Product Cycle, *Quarterly Journal of Economics*, 80, 1966, pp. 190–207.
Wu, J. C., Telecom Sector Expands International Cooperation, *Beijing Review*, June 26-July 2, 1995.
Yamin, M., An Evolutionary Analysis of Subsidiary Innovation and 'Reverse' Transfer in Multinational Companies, in Macharzina, K./Oesterle, M. J./Wolf, J. (eds), *Global Business in the Information Age*, Proceedings of the 23rd Annual EIBA Conference, Stuttgart, December 14–16, 1997, pp. 211–230.
Yin, R. K., *Case Study Research: Design and Methods*, 2nd edition, London: Sage 1994.
Zhu, G./Speece, M. W./So, S. L. M., Conflicts in Sino-European Joint Ventures, in Selmes, J. (ed), *International Management in China: Cross-Cultural Issues*, London: Routledge 1998, pp. 13–28.

Management International Review

Neuerscheinungen

Joachim Scholz
Wert und Bewertung internationaler Akquisitionen
2001
XXII, 365 S. mit 40 Abb.,
(mir-Edition),
Br. € 79,–
ISBN 3-409-11602-8

Joachim Wolf
Strategie und Struktur 1955–1995: Ein Kapitel der Geschichte deutscher nationaler und internationaler Unternehmen
2000
XXXII, 673 S. mit 156 Abb.,
7 farb. Abb. (mir-Edition),
Br. € 94,50
ISBN 3-409-11637-0

Dodo zu Knyphausen-Aufseß (Hrsg.)
Globalisierung als Herausforderung der Betriebswirtschaftslehre
2000
XVIII, 285 S. (mir-Edition),
Br. € 64,–
ISBN 3-409-11719-9

Laila Maija Hofmann
Führungskräfte in Europa. Empirische Analyse zukünftiger Anforderungen
2000
XXVIII, 414 S. mit 89 Abb.,
129 Tab., Diss. Augsburg 2000
(mir-Edition),
Br. € 64,–
ISBN 3-409-11704-0

Frank Niederländer
Dynamik in der internationalen Produktpolitik von Automobilherstellern
2000
XXVIII, 296 S. mit 111 Abb.,
36 Tab., Dissertation Eichstätt 2000
(mir-Edition),
Br. € 59,–
ISBN 3-409-11722-9

Jan Hendrik Fisch
Structure Follows Knowledge. Internationale Verteilung der Forschung und Entwicklung in multinationalen Unternehmen
2001
XXII, 247 S. mit 84 Abb., 10 Tab.
(mir-Edition),
Br. € 49,–
ISBN 3-409-11802-0

Betriebswirtschaftlicher Verlag Dr. Th. Gabler GmbH, Abraham-Lincoln-Str. 46, 65189 Wiesbaden

Fiona Moore

Internal Diversity and Culture's Consequences: Branch/Head Office Relations in a German Financial MNC

Abstract

- The different subcultures within the branches of MNCs have as much impact on its functioning as the corporation's home and host cultures, but are less likely to be considered significant.

- Taking as a case study the matrix integration of the London branch of a German MNC, I examine the reasons for, and results of, its managers' failure to take this internal diversity into account.

Key Results

- The internal diversity of MNCs is key both to the corporation's functioning and to the success of mergers and restructurings.

Author

Fiona Moore, Postdoctoral Researcher, Said Business School, University of Oxford, Oxford UK.

Fiona Moore

Introduction

Since the 1980s, much has been written on the cultural issues surrounding the relationship between the head offices of multinational corporations (MNCs) and their branches. Few writers, however, have considered the implications of the fact that each branch also contains within itself diverse groups, each with their own interests, strategies and agendas. Through a case study of the implementation of a matrix integration programme in the London branch of a German multinational bank, I shall examine the impact of intrabranch (as opposed to interbranch) diversity on an MNC.

Many writers in management studies have debated the question of whether a branch's home or host culture has the most influence on its cultural makeup. The simplest view portrays the corporation as a more or less integral unit, whose interests are largely dictated by Head Office (Bergsten et al. 1978). Branches, while they may have superficial regional differences, are said to take the head office, rather than the local culture, as their main influence (van Magren/Laurent 1993, p. 304); they are seen as "colonies," as it were, of the head office (Fröbel/Heinrichs/Kreye 1980). However, this approach has been criticised for ignoring the fact that branches have of necessity to adapt to local conditions (Child/Kieser 1979, pp. 252–260). It is thus difficult to claim that the sole influence upon the branches of MNCs is the home culture of their Head Offices.

Proponents of the "national business systems" approach (e.g. Whitley 1992), by contrast, prioritise the influence of the branch's host culture over that of the home culture on its makeup. Taking Hofstede's classic study of cultural difference between employees of the branches of an MNC, *Culture's Consequences*, as a starting point, supporters of this view argue that branches are socially disparate parts of the wider organization, which bring local expertise to the corporation as a whole (Hofstede 1980, Mueller 1994, p. 408, Andersson et al. 2001, p. 1014). One should thus consider MNCs less as single entities, and more as collections of groups with diverse needs (Streeck 1996, Hofstede 1980, p. 381). This approach has, however, come into question, as other studies have demonstrated that in fact the culture of a corporation's head office can be a major influence on its branches (Mueller 1994, p. 408). Furthermore, although Hofstede acknowledged that there were other influences on branches than simply the host culture, the scope of his study does not permit him to develop this (1980, p. 105); subsequent writers have consequently glossed over the influences of other sorts of culture, and have frequently, through their efforts to develop a counterargument to the "home country" stance discussed above, focused their arguments more or less exclusively on branch culture to a sometimes unrealistic degree (Mueller 1994, p. 407). Although the host culture has an undeniable presence, then, it is not the only thing affecting the branches of MNCs.

The most complex approach has been to take a stance which acknowledges influences from both sources. Mueller argues that "country-specific patterns . . . interact with company-specific patterns to form varying blends" (1994, p. 40). Ghoshal and Nohria propose a set of four distinct ways in which branches and head offices interact, depending on the subsidiary's environment and the corporation's needs (1989); while one might question whether four is the most accurate number, it is indubitable that there are a number of different ways in which a branch's culture can relate to that of the organisation as a whole. Kristensen and Zeitlin (2001)'s ongoing studies of dairy-product MNCs show that not only do the branches have their own goals and objectives within the organisation, but that there are marked differences between those branches which were set up as foreign wings of a particular corporation and those which were formerly independent companies acquired through takeovers or mergers. The most comprehensive writing on the subject thus suggests a diversity of influences upon the cultural makeup of branches.

Despite this, however, none of the studies mentioned above take into account the question of intrabranch diversity. While Kristensen and Zeitlin refer to company-wide internal power struggles (2001), the other writers focus on the interaction between corporate and local culture with regard to the branch's relationship with head office. Furthermore, it is becoming increasingly obvious that to ignore this diversity is to ignore a crucial aspect of organization: not only are the particular relationships which different groups have with the home and host cultures ignored, and branch employees made subject to the same treatment by Head Office, regardless of whether it is right for their situation, the considerable strategic advantages of having a workforce with diverse cultural links are unexplored. Although it has been acknowledged that branches are not undifferentiated units, and actually contain many groups with diverse interests, then, the impact of this on the branch's culture and relationship with Head Office has seldom been explored.

Methodology

This project is based on an ethnographic study which was carried out at a German multinational bank between January and June 2000, with follow-up work done between July 2000 and January 2001, as part of an eighteen-month study of German bank branches in London, England. Ethnographic fieldwork involves a qualitative, first-person approach, focusing less on quantitative data such as statistics and more on interviews and observation. While this approach has been criticized for the difficulty in generalizing from the results thereby obtained, it has proved useful in addressing questions of culture which are hard to understand in quantifiable terms; furthermore, the researcher does not work with predefined variables and categories, but lets the phenomena studied determine the focus of the material (Harris 2000, p. 755–776, Chapman 1997, p. 11). As we are here considering the lived experience of an MNC's culture, rather than drawing cross-cultural generalizations according to a predetermined framework, an ethnographic approach will be used in preference to more statistical ones.

The material on which this paper is based consists of, firstly, six months' worth of observation of and participation in the office environment, which involved coming in to the bank every working day and having access to a desk in a shared office, the canteen and other basic staff resources, and meeting rooms in which to conduct interviews. The location of the desk changed three times over the six-month period, allowing me to see different parts of the organization in action.

Formal interviews were conducted on a periodic basis over the course of the six-month participant-observation period and the six months following it, with sixteen individuals at the London branch. Of these, six were expatriate Germans, five were Germans living permanently in the UK, two were English who had lived in Germany, and three were English with no German connection. The people interviewed were mainly junior and middle managers, with three members of top management and two non-managerial staff members also participating. In addition, formal interviews of this type were conducted at the bank's Head Office with six managers in the personnel department and one in a Front Office division; these were conducted during three trips to Frankfurt, in April, September and October of 2000, with follow-up work done via telephone and e-mail. Each participant was interviewed between one and four times, with interviews lasting approximately an hour apiece. Although a standard questionnaire was used to start the interview, it was normally abandoned early on, with the interests of the interview subject being allowed to shape the proceedings. Bilingual interviewees were given the option of being interviewed in English or German; although most at the London Branch chose English, and most at the Head Office chose German, no interview was conducted exclusively in one or the other language, as participants would occasionally drop into the other language for expressions that they felt unable to translate, or if they found giving an explanation in a language which was not their mother tongue too difficult.

These interviews were also complemented by informal interviews and conversations with about twenty other members of the branch's staff. These followed no set pattern, although I made certain to ask whether or not I could use the relevant part of the conversation in my study, and were usually conducted over lunch or after work. Informal interviews of this sort were held with all but four of the formal-interview participants; of the other people with whom I regularly had conversations of this sort, five were Germans living permanently in the UK, six were non-Germans who had lived in Germany, and nine were non-German employees with no connection to Germany.

My position with regard to the bank was as an outside consultant to the London branch, brought in to advise, based on my interview results, on the impact of the matrix integration programme on Anglo-German relations in the branch. I was expected to submit a report at the end of the first six months detailing the issues in this area which had arisen from the matrix integration and suggesting solutions. Interviewees were thus aware that the results of their interviews might find their way – albeit anonymously – into the final report; I have tried to compensate for this by evaluating each interviewee's answers in the context of their political agenda with regard to the bank and the matrix integration programme, and thus to factor their individual biases into the report.

This project was, therefore, conducted using ethnographic research methods while the researcher acted as consultant on Anglo-German cultural issues to the bank in question. This approach was judged to provide a solid basis from which to examine the lived experience of culture in the London branch of a German financial corporation.

Four Into One: The Culture of London Branch

In order to investigate the impact of internal differences on the multinational corporation, we must first define what exactly this internal differentiation consists of in this case. In this section, therefore, I will be describing the bank which is the setting of the study, its London office and the different groups which can be found there.

The bank in question is a Frankfurt-based universal bank which, while it is one of the largest banks of its kind in Germany and maintains an above-average number of foreign branches, is still fairly limited in its international operations, a not-atypical state of affairs in German banking (as noted in Ebster-Grosz/Pugh 1996). It has maintained a presence in London since the early 1970s, with a full branch being opened in 1981. The longest-serving employee (a senior manager) had been with London Branch for fifteen years at the time of the study, the shortest-serving (a trainee), three months. The branch had about 160 staff members, including trainee, temporary and service employees (the latter frequently being on contract from other organisations). Of these, about one-third were German, Swiss or Austrian, one-tenth were non-German foreign staff (mainly from former colonies of the United Kingdom) and the rest originated from the United Kingdom. Contrary to the usual pattern for German overseas bank branches, in which the German staff tend to be concentrated in the upper echelons (Arthur D. Little Ltd. 1979, p. 73), the Germans were fairly evenly distributed throughout the bank. The focus of the bank as a whole is on the German market, with London

Branch's main function being to serve its clients' overseas offices. When described according to its population and market position, then, London Branch appears to be a social unit with a single definite ethnic division, a common history and a particular relationship with Head Office.

Beneath the surface, however, four social groups could be discerned within the branch. These groups were identified over the course of the formal and informal interviews mentioned above, as I noted that particular patterns of association between ethnic origin, length of residence in England, and their position with regard to Head Office seemed to emerge among my interviewees. I also noticed that branch employees also seemed to speak, in interviews and in conversation, in terms of the branch as being socially divided between German and non-German staff, and in terms of these being further divided into two groups based on their social proximity to Germany, and that individuals tended to associate, broadly speaking, with other individuals of similar national origin and degree of association with England vis-à-vis Germany. We shall here call these groups "cohorts," in order to avoid confusion with any other sort of social group which may be referred to in this paper.

The first cohort consisted of the branch's German expatriates. These were primarily specialists who, like the elite labour migrants described by such researchers as Anne-Wil Harzing (1999) and, in a more ethnographic vein, J. V. Beaverstock (1991, 1996), had been brought over from Head Office to fill a new post or to ease a department through a transition period, usually for between one and three years. All had at least a vocational-college education; most were in their thirties, had spent seven to nine years at Head Office, and, with one or two exceptions, had prior experience of living, studying and/or working in London. All had volunteered to be there, mainly to gain international experience and/or to "see the world." They were strongly associated with Head Office by colleagues, and still maintained strong social connections with it. The expatriates thus had a particular stance with regard to Head Office and the local culture, which no other group within the branch was in a position to share.

The second cohort consisted of locally hired Germans. These were fairly diverse in terms of age, background and length of time at London Branch, but all were living in England permanently for one reason or other which was not business-related: an English spouse, for instance, or a sense of estrangement from German society. They tended to be more oriented to UK than to Head Office business practices and culture, and were seen by many UK employees as "more like Anglo-Saxons than the other Germans," as one Southern English manager put it. Most have worked at other (frequently, though not always, German) City of London institutions before coming to London Branch; all make a point of identification of being fluently multilingual, and do not show any particular solidarity with the expatriates. The locally hired Germans are thus more distant from Head Office and closer to UK business culture than the expatriates.

The third cohort was the "Germanophiles": non-German staff members who felt a strong connection with Germany and its culture, and who spoke the language with relative fluency. This group was varied, including as it did people with German partners, ethnic Germans born elsewhere, and people who had been sent on staff exchanges to Head Office. Some had joined the bank due to their interest in Germany, while others had acquired their interest due to their work at the bank. Most had university degrees, and tended to socialise primarily with each other and with locally hired German staff. However, most expressed an ambivalence with regard to Head Office; while participants in staff exchanges did express more sympathy with its problems in dealing with branches than did other non-Germans, they tended also to be critical of Head Office policies. As was the case with the German staff, some non-German staff at London Branch were closer to German business culture than others.

The final cohort is that of the "Anglophiles": locally hired, mainly English, staff with no particular connection to Germany beyond their having been hired by this particular corporation. This is not to say that they bear any particular dislike for Germany, but that they were not as strongly oriented towards it as were other groups. They tended to conform more with UK business norms; few had university or vocational-college degrees. Most also spoke of Head Office as an external force, an outside entity with a totally separate culture. They were, however, no less globally oriented than other cohorts with more obvious connections outside the UK, frequently travelling or having worked abroad, or having relatives and friends in other countries. The Anglophiles were thus more distant to Head Office, and closer to London, than the other groups.

While a traditional view of the organization might suggest that the most important dynamic is that between London Branch/UK culture and Head Office/German culture, an examination of London Branch suggests that there are, in fact, several different groups with different relationships to Head Office and to German culture in general within it. It remains to be seen, however, how these divisions affect the branch at times of change.

Divided Loyalties: The Matrix Integration of London Branch

At the time of this study, the bank had embarked upon a restructuring programme aimed at imposing a more transnational structure on the bank – referred to as the "matrix integration programme"–which it had almost completed by the time I left (see Hofstede 1980, pp. 385–386). While conflict between different factions of employees seems to be an inevitable part of any restructuring (see Cody 1990), here, the presence of ethnically-based cohorts within the branch was largely ignored in favour of a cultural integration plan which targeted supposed national differences between branch and head office.

From its establishment until July 1999, London Branch had operated more or less autonomously from the rest of the bank. It retained a traditional "pyramid structure," in which the heads of individual departments reported to the General Manager, who was the only staff member in regular contact with superiors in Frankfurt. Under the matrix integration system, however, individual department heads reported directly to individual departmental superiors in Frankfurt, making the bank's structure less a matter of individual national branches reporting to a centre in Frankfurt, as of globe-spanning departments radiating out from Frankfurt, causing a shift from a multidomestic to a "transnational" business strategy (see Ghoshal/Bartlett 1989, pp. 15–20). Consequently, many London Branch staff members who had previously had little to do with the Frankfurt office now found themselves reporting to a German "global head," and there was an increased presence of visitors, expatriate employees and others associated with Head Office at the branch; in addition, many employees had to learn particular business practices which were commonly used at Head Office, but were less often seen in London. The new initiative thus entailed a change from a structure focused on national units to one focused on a Frankfurt-centred global network.

In London Branch, a number of problems arose from the integration, mostly relating to employees having difficulty learning the new business practices, or to the fact that many failed to use the new reporting system, continuing instead to use the old structure. In addition, a sense of hostility between branch and Head Office developed, with London employees expressing fears that Head Office would restructure the bank along lines which were useful to its own purposes, but ultimately detrimental to the functioning of London Branch. Although such tensions do not seem directly related to national identity, they were described to me exclusively as relating to differences in national business culture. Many employees spoke of practical problems of adjusting London Branch to the (German) business system of Head Office; I was, as I said above, brought in specifically to report on "the problem" of "the differences between UK and German business cultures," by which managers appeared to mean that they perceived resistance on the part of non-German and some of the more locally integrated German employees to learning German business practices, and difficulties on the part of more recent arrivals of learning UK business practices. A number of Londoners took advantage of the situation to learn German at corporate expense, which was described by some as a smart business move and by others as "sucking up" to Head Office; both views again define the key tension at issue as one of national culture. Consequently, both the extant and anticipated tensions with regard to the matrix integration were seen in terms of clashes between two national business cultures brought together in an organization.

Within London Branch, however, the four cohorts discussed above also had different positions vis-à-vis the branch and the Head Office. The German expatriates had all been sent from Head Office to ease key departments into the transition, and consequently presented themselves as forming a bridge between Head Office and London Branch. At the time there were no other expatriates, bar a few who had stayed on for ten or more years and become socially reclassified, as it were, as "local hires." Most of them described the initiative in terms of the formerly-independent London being brought into line with Head Office. They also noted that the reporting structure brought in by the initiative is not new for them as it is to others in the branch. While one or two questioned the applicability of Head Office's structure to the much smaller branch, none suggested that the integration programme should therefore be modified or abandoned, instead concentrating on ways of making the two structures compatible; one said that his London staff had "a lot of learning to do," rather than suggest that Head Office, or he himself, might equally be in need of developing outside knowledge. The expatriates thus described themselves as interpreters, linking Head Office to London Branch.

The locally hired Germans, by contrast, focused on ground-level conflict in London rather than on abstract talk of bridging cultures. The matrix integration was discussed in terms of changes it would bring to their particular departments, rather than as affecting the branch or bank as a whole. When they discussed questions of UK versus German business culture, it was usually in terms of specific cases and individuals; they tended to express frustration with both Anglophiles and recent German expatriates' difficulties in understanding each others' viewpoints, and tended to voice more concerns about Anglophile colleagues' lack of foreign language skills than did other groups. Many also took pains to stress that their ethnic identity did not necessarily make them partial to Head Office; members of this group often began discussions of Head Office practices with the phrase "While I'm German, I disapprove . . ." The locally hired Germans thus, like the expatriates, portrayed their role as one of interpreting between cultures; the local hires, however, focused on specific incidents and ground-level impacts upon London Branch rather than talking in broad, abstract terms. They also took pains to emphasise that being German did not automatically dispose one positively towards Head Office culture.

The Germanophiles, hence, interpreted the situation in terms not so much of conflicting national cultures, as in terms of cosmopolitanism versus parochiality. Problems with the matrix integration were usually attributed to lack of familiarity with other cultures on the part of both Head Office and London staff. The Germanophiles were strongly critical of Head Office for, in their opinion, imposing a new set of rules and nomenclature on the branch without consulting those directly affected; however, they were equally critical of Anglophile managers for not taking advantage of company-sponsored programmes which would allow them to spend time in Head Office, learn German and/or become more familiar with the culture (by which, interestingly, they appeared to mean that of the wider German society as well as simply its business systems), one saying "I'm not going to force people, but you should at least *go*, and see what they say in Head Office. . . it's not going to just happen, you have to make it happen." Their criticisms in all cases focused on their perception that both groups were "taking a local perspective" and not considering the wider consequences. The Germanophiles, then, focused not so much on conflict between German and UK business cultures as they did on "local people" failing to take a global perspective.

The Anglophiles, lastly, tended to present the situation in terms of a hostile foreign culture imposing itself upon an embattled local culture. Most emphasised London's formerly isolated status, saying that Head Office had until recently left them to their own devices. Consequently, they described the integration in terms of loss of UK culture to an outside body with a very different way of acting:

> What we've got here is a structure which derived from Head Office – in a branch. Which is in my judgement organised as if it were part of the Head Office. You've got a bunch of people in a different country, with a different character and background, and a different sort of – a different *understanding* of the way business functions. (Senior manager, English)

The Anglophiles thus described the initiative not so much in terms of bridging gaps between national business cultures, ground-level conflict between colleagues or of cosmopolitan versus local perspectives, but as the imposition of one business culture upon another, whose members perceived it as vulnerable to being overwhelmed.

The branch which appears to be unified on one level, therefore, in fact includes within it several different subgroups, each with a slightly different position with regard to Head Office and the matrix integration, due to differences between their positions and career perspectives within the company, their linguistic makeups, their members' life histories, and other factors. The expatriates spoke in terms of broad differences between national business cultures and the need to bridge the gap between Head Office and London Branch; the local hires focused instead on the day-to-day problems of individuals adjusting to a new system, distancing themselves from Head Office as they did so. The Germanophiles, by contrast, focus on the globalisation aspects of the issue, presenting the problem less as one of national cultures and more of lack of cosmopolitanism. Finally, the Anglophiles present the situation almost as one of cultural imperialism on the part of Head Office. Although one might, broadly speaking, argue that all the issues stem from the fact that a German Head Office was brought into closer contact with its UK branch, in practice each of the cohorts has slightly different issues within this remit, which divided the branch internally. The result of this was the expression of a good deal of inter-cohort suspicion – as each suspected the other of either being partisan to or resistant to Head Office, depending on their feelings towards it – which made for less easy acceptance of the matrix integration, and unnecessary friction between colleagues and departments, as different individuals were suspected or, occasionally, accused, rightly or wrongly, of adopting a position which was unpopular with another group.

The differences in interpretation also reflect diverse agendas within the initiative. While there is a common concept of German business culture, for instance, the cohorts with more of an interest in staying close to Head Office tend to have a more positive interpretation of the initiative than those with more London-focused interests. Similarly, those cohorts which are betwixt and between the English and German business cultures – the Germanophiles and the locally hired Germans – are safeguarding their positions by downplaying the possibility of interpreting the conflicts as the result of a simple English/German opposition. Although these different agendas could not be said to totally disrupt the restructuring, they did lead to increased tension and lack of communication; several of the expatriates commented that the local hires and Anglophiles were not willing to talk freely around them, and interviewees from all cohorts generally evinced a lack of sympathy for the issues of other cohorts when these were raised in interviews. Many of my informal interviews, for instance, were initiated by a staff member approaching me during a break and telling me an anecdote about their frustration in working with some colleague from another cohort, ranging from mild (a Germanophile laughing over an Anglophile's inability to speak German) to severe (an Anglophile expressing the fear that they would be "promoted sideways" in favour of an expatriate). The cohorts were thus divided along the lines of their interests in the organisation.

The sense of hostility and occasional intergroup conflicts which London Branch experienced as a part of the matrix integration therefore did not stem particularly from the irreconcilability of Head Office practices with the London business environment, as both offices had been mediating the two systems for decades. Rather, these problems stemmed from the unacknowledged fact that there were at least four different interest groups within London Branch, each with a different position relative to Head Office and to the other groups, and a different aim with regard to its objectives in the restructuring of the bank. As a consequence, there was an increased level of suspicion within the workplace, as well as mounting distrust on the part of all groups (including some of the expatriates) for the aims of Head Office.

The View from Frankfurt: Relations between Head Office and London Branch

The view from Head Office, however, was somewhat different. In Frankfurt, the issues arising from the matrix integration were seen exclusively in terms of branch versus Head Office, and of UK culture versus German. Head Office's difficulties in understanding the situation at London Branch thus stem from too great a focus on cultural differences as opposed to considering the impact of the presence of local subgroups on the branch.

Head Office consists of a complex of modern buildings close to the centre of Frankfurt. It employs approximately two thousand staff in total, with all staff members pertaining to particular departments generally being housed in the same area of the complex, but in separate, enclosed offices containing two or three people rather than the big open-plan offices of London Branch. A recent expatriate to London described it by saying that "it's just like head offices, it's a lot of politics in the organisation, very bureaucratic . . . in Head Office I would be one of many, but here I am just one." There were fewer non-German staff in Head Office than there were non-English staff in London. While I could not obtain educational statistics on Head Office, I spoke with a number of people there who held postgraduate degrees, including doctorates, which was almost unheard-of in London; this appears to be partly due to a higher valuation of qualifications over experience on the part of German businesses, and partly to the fact that Head Office's more specialised functions necessitated more highly trained personnel. Head Office thus is much larger, less diverse and more focused on formal qualifications than is London Branch; its employees are thus starting from a very different position than their London counterparts with regard to understanding the organisation.

As in London, the staff members at Head Office with whom I spoke described cultural issues within the bank very much in terms of home versus host cultures. London, one said, may be a big branch within the organisation, but the main reference point of the bank is Germany. When discussing the overseas branches, Head Office employees tended to speak of these as outposts which were, firstly, opposed to Head Office, and secondly, were integral, undifferentiated units. Branches were perceived to be strongly oriented to their particular regions, and described in terms of their "national" cultures. One manager spoke disparagingly of "regional princes" who run branches according to their own agendas. Head Office was said to take a global, and branches a local, perspective; one personnel manager from Head Office described the London Branch as important to the banking system simply because a lot of German businesses operate in the UK, rather than due to its location in a "global city" with connections all over the world. Another said that local influence was what distinguished the branches from Head Office. The branches are thus described at Head Office as single units, taking a local perspective.

The matrix integration, similarly, was described in terms of incorporating solidary units of "foreign culture" into the "German culture" of Head Office. Most people at Head Office spoke of the need to "integrate the overseas branches into the system," on the grounds that they were isolated from the culture of Head Office. One personnel manager said that the aim of expatriation – and in particular the increase in expatriate numbers during the matrix integration – was to instil better knowledge of Head Office practices in the branches (see Edstrom/Galbraith 1977); there was never any discussion of the possibility of the two systems co-existing. The expatriates were, furthermore, expected to replace "local" practices with ones compatible to Head Office's. Finally, other possible influences on the branch (establishment mode, for instance) were never acknowledged. The matrix integration was thus discussed, not only in ways which assumed the branches to be monocultural, but which assumed that the branches must be either dominated by the local or the bank's home culture.

Consequently, London Branch's difficulties in adjusting to the new practices brought about by the matrix integration were discussed at Head Office in terms of branches, dominated by their host cultures, resisting the imposition of the home culture. One of the heads of the integration project said that her impression was that the branches felt that Head Office was imposing its business culture on their local practices, and that they were expressing anti-German feeling as a result – a curious impression when one considers that this applied, in London, only to the Anglophiles. Head Office managers thus described the branches in ways which assumed that the problems of integration came from the resistance of the branch as a whole to outside cultural imposition.

This idea appears to stem at least partly from lack of personal experience with branch culture. Of the personnel managers with whom I spoke, only one had actually participated in the expatriate programme. Contact with foreign branches is, moreover, organised by a specific section of the personnel department with a particular responsibility for this, and its members are the ones who have the most to do with selection and preparation of expatriates. Outside of this section, few in Head Office seemed to have much contact with, or even be aware of, current and/or former expatriates. This impression of distance was echoed by London Branch employees. While relations with Head Office were not unpleasant, London staff usually described Head Office as having maintained a hands-off policy for the most part prior to the matrix integration; some employees continued to speak of it as if it were another bank. One Germanophile explicitly said that, in his opinion "this [matrix integration] is like a foreign takeover." While it is not true to say that there was negligible contact between the institutions prior to the integration – as a large minority of London Branch staff had participated in courses or exchanges, and one or two actually "commuted" between the offices on a weekly basis – the percentage of staff who participated in such programmes is relatively larger in London than in Frankfurt. London Branch thus has more awareness of Head Office's culture than Head Office has of the situation at London Branch.

Most of my Head Office interviewees had, however, some degree of familiarity with management-studies theories on the subject of the influences of home and host cultures on multinational corporations. Hofstede was continually referenced, both explicitly and implicitly, in personnel department workshops on how the matrix integration would affect the bank; one division had even developed a computer game, based on *Culture's Consequences*, in which the user could fill out a Hofstede questionnaire to discover which "national culture" best fit an individual or company (Hofstede 1980). Hofstede was continually invoked as a guideline for explaining the differences, and the sources of friction, between the Head Office and London Branch. In the absence of direct experience, then, Hofstede's findings were embraced as means of explaining and resolving issues.

There are, nonetheless, some significant differences between the way in which the book in question is written, and how it is interpreted. While Hofstede acknowledges throughout his work that multinational corporations are internally divided along other lines than cultural ones (1980; see, for instance, p. 105), the interpretation which the personnel managers drew from *Culture's Consequences* seemed to be, firstly, that branches are cultural units, secondly, that the host cultures of branches are also undifferentiated units, and, thirdly, that national cultural differences are the only ones of relevance to the matrix integration (as opposed to, say, age of branch, ethnic composition, establishment mode, and so forth). Anecdotal evidence suggests, furthermore, that many of the people who cited Hofstede had not in fact read the original work, but were quoting secondary or tertiary sources. Throughout the integration process, then, the branches have been regarded as single, solidary units, rather than as dynamic entities which are divided along several internal lines, due to the common interpretation of Hofstede as a literal description of branch/Head Office relations rather than an academic monograph.

The consequences for the integration of London Branch are thus plain. Firstly, if the branch is considered to be a unit, all sections and employees will receive more or less the same prescribed treatment, regardless of whether or not this addresses their issues. Secondly, the fact that the branch is not universally opposed to Head Office goes unacknowledged, meaning that, as individuals sympathetic to Head Office become alienated by the constant assumption that they are in opposition to it, a culture of mutual hostility develops; several of the expatriates, who had started out expressing their eagerness to help London integrate with Head Office, were to be heard expressing open criticism later on in their tenure, and Head Office people, for their part, tended to regard the local knowledge picked up by expatriates as idiosyncrasies requiring elimination. Thirdly, it means that the bank as a whole fails to capitalise on the internal diversity within the branches. By conceiving of the organisation not in terms of diverse cohorts of different degrees of social proximity to Head Office, but as national units, the organisation may in fact be creating rather than solving its problems.

In sum, then, the lack of direct experience of branch culture, coupled with the common interpretation of Hofstede as a guidebook rather than an academic work, mean that the view from Head Office is one which focuses on national culture rather than internal diversity. Had a different interpretation of the branch and the management-studies literature been embraced, the integration might have proceeded more smoothly.

Summary and Conclusions: Banking On Culture

The main issue regarding London Branch's ability to adjust to the changes brought about by the matrix integration programme is thus, contrary to much of the previous work done on the subject, not so much the differences in national business culture between London Branch and Head Office as the presence of different groups within the branch with different perspectives on, and different agendas regarding, the organisation. This is not to say that the difference in "national business systems" has had no impact on the integration, but it cannot be ignored that an equal and possibly greater factor influencing the exercise is the different perspectives and strategies of cohorts within individual branches and even Head Office itself. This goes unacknowledged at all levels of the organisation, creating problems when attempts are made to integrate the MNC into a global network without addressing these issues. There is therefore a need to perceive cultural differences, not as static givens, but as dynamic concepts which vary in degree, intensity and aim depending on social factors within and outside the organisation.

Furthermore, although in this case it led to increased tension levels and conflict between parts of the organization, the presence of different groups is not a bad thing, and in fact is a potential source of strength in cases such as the one discussed here. The Germanophiles who had been on exchanges to Head Office, for instance, could not only mediate between the offices, but also make Head Office seem a less alien place to coworkers; the German local hires could provide a more general perspective on the issues of moving between UK and German cultures, where the globally-focused viewpoint of the Anglophiles could challenge Head Office's images of branches as parochial. Furthermore, by reconceiving the branch not so much in explicit ethnic terms as in terms of belonging to diverse groups with different degrees of engagement with Head Office, the sense of hostility which periodically emerged between English and German employees in London could be reduced. The diversity of the organization, if recognized, could therefore be one of its strengths with regard to the matrix integration.

Much of the difficulty in recognizing this, furthermore, seems to stem from the simplified view of Hofstede's study adopted by many of the managers in the organisation, frequently via the work of popular business writers. It does have to be acknowledged that this process is to some degree inevitable; stereotyping and the development of collective "myths" are well-known to be a part of group formation (Czarniawska 1997); note, for instance, the construction of the "problem" of "the differences between UK and German business structures," which seemed to be more about defining the organization's identity than about any real difficulties in this regard. However, in this instance it would seem that the result has been the production of hostility between two groups which should be working together, and the waste of potential resources and usable skills. It would not necessarily be difficult to develop a collective myth which acknowledges greater diversity within the organisation, and it is possible that, as the current generation of academic literature is adopted by the popular business press, this will develop; for the time being, however, undue hostility has been the result in at least one corporation.

Furthermore, this case has implications for theorizing about the internal integration and diversity of the MNC. Although "home" and "host" cultures do have an influence on MNCs in a variety of different ways, it appears that different groups within the organization have different degrees and kinds of relationship with the home and host cultures, as implied in Kristensen and Zeitlin (2001) and Mueller (1994), depending on national origin, ethnic composition, establishment mode and so forth. It also seems that to consider branches and Head Offices as integral social units is to miss out on the potentially very influential internal divisions within these, which Hofstede hinted at but never fully developed. Finally, the fact that the local hires took pains to highlight differences in opinion between them and other Germans at the branch suggests that it is not "national culture" as such which is at issue here, but something more complex. It might, therefore, be better to think of branches not simply as nodes in a global network, but as networks in and of themselves, with diverse interests and influences coming to play on different groups every bit as much as in the wider network of the corporation.

In order for this premise to be developed further, then, more research needs to be done on the social makeup of branches, and the implications of this for their relationships with Head Office. A longer-term study, which took in more branches and developed a more extensive treatment of the culture of Head Office, would be ideal, perhaps involving a team of researchers, or something along the lines of Kristensen and Zeitlin's ten-year-long periodic study of the same companies. It might also be worth comparing this branch to other subsidiaries which developed from specialised local companies later acquired by the bank in question.

In sum, the case of the matrix integration of a German bank branch in the City of London does more than suggest that there is greater internal diversity within MNCs than previous studies have acknowledged. By highlighting the fact that branches are not integral social units, but are made up of diverse groups with different relations to the corporation's home and host culture, it suggests that it may be better to conceive of MNCs as networks within networks rather than as linked groups of solidary entities.

References

Andersson, U./ Fosgren, M./ Holm, U., Subsidiary Embeddedness and Competence Development in MNCs: A Multi-Level Analysis, *Organization Studies* 22, 6, 2001, pp. 1013–1034.

Arthur D. Little Ltd., *The EEC as an Expanded Home Market for the United Kingdom and the Federal Republic of Germany*, London: Anglo-German Foundation 1979.

Beaverstock, J. V., Skilled International Migration: an Analysis of the Geography of International Secondments within Large Accountancy Firms, *Environment and Planning*, 23, 1991, pp. 1133–1146.
Beaverstock, J. V., Migration, Knowledge and Social Interaction: Expatriate Labour within Investment Banks, *Area*, 28, 4, 1996, pp. 459–470.
Bergsten, C. F. et al., *American Multinationals and American Interests*, Washington: The Brookings Institution 1978.
Chapman, M., Preface: Social Anthropology, Business Studies and Cultural Issues, *Inernational Studies of Management and Organization*, 26, 4, 1997, pp. 3–29.
Child, J./Kieser, A., Organization and Managerial Roles in British and West German Companies, in Lammers, C. J./Hickson, D. J. (eds.), *Organizations Alike and Unalike: International and Inter-Institutional Studies in the Sociology of Organizations*, London: Routledge 1979, pp. 251–271.
Cody, T., *Strategy of a Megamerger*, New York: Quorum Books 1990.
Czarniawska, B., *Narrating the Organization: Dramas of Institutional Identity*, London: University of Chicago Press 1997.
Ebster-Grosz, D./Pugh, D., *Anglo-German Business Collaboration: Pitfalls and Potentials*, London: MacMillan Press 1996.
Edstrom, Anders/Galbraith, Jay R., Transfer of Managers as a Coordination and Control Strategy in Multinational Organizations, *Administrative Science Quarterly*, 22, 2, 1977, pp. 248–264
Fröbel, F./Heinrichs, J/Kreye, O., *The New International Division of Labour: Structural Unemployment in Industrialized Countries*, translated by P. Burgess, Cambridge: Cambridge University Press 1980.
Ghoshal, S/Bartlett, C. A., *Managing Across Borders: The Transnational Solution*, 2nd editon, London: Random House 1998
Ghoshal, S./Nohria, N., Internal Differentiation within Multinational Corporations, *Strategic Management Journal* 10, 1989, pp. 323–32.
Harris, S., Reconciling Positive and Interpretative Inernational Management Research: A Native Category Approach, *Internatinal Business Review* 9, 2000, pp. 755–770.
Harzing, A.-W., *Of Bumble-bees and Spiders: the Role of Expatriates in Controlling Foreign Subsidiaries*, University of Bradford Management Centre Working Paper no. 9822, Bradford: University of Bradford 1999
Hickson, D. J./Pugh, D. S., *Management Worldwide: The Impact of Societal Culture on Organizations around the Globe*, London: Penguin 1997.
Hofstede, G., *Culture's Consequences: International Differences in Work-Related Values*, London: Sage, 1980.
Kristensen, P. H./Zeitlin, J., *A Global Game Enacted By Local Players: Subsidiaries, Headquarters, And The Strategic Constitution Of A Multinational Corporation*, Paper presented at the ESRC Transnational Communities Programme Conference "Multinational Enterprises: Embedded Organisations, Transnational Federations, or Global Learning Communities?", Arden House, University of Warwick, Coventry, September 6–8, 2001.
Mueller, F., "Societal Effect, Organizational Effect and Globalization", *Organization Studies*, 15, 3, 1994, pp. 407–28.
Streeck, W., Lean Production in the German Auto Industry: A Test Case for Convergence Theory, in Berger, S./Dore, R. (eds.), *National Diversity and Global Capitalism*, London: Cornell 1996, pp. 138–170.
van Magren, J./Laurent, A., The Multinational Corporation as an Interorganizational Network, in Ghoshal, S./Westney, D. E. (eds.), *Organization Theory and the Multinational Corporation*, London: The MacMillan Press, 1993, pp. 275–309.
Whitley, R., Societies, Firms and Markets: the Social Structuring of Business Systems, in Whitley, R. (ed.), *European Business Systems: Firms and Markets in their National Contexts*, London: Sage 1992, pp. 5–45

mir *Edition*

Jan Hendrik Fisch

Structure Follows Knowledge

International Distribution of Research and Development in Multinational Corporations

2001, XXII, 247 pages, Br., € 49,00 (approx. US $ 45.–)
ISBN 3-409-11802-0

While the general factors influencing the internationalization of research and development are well-known, there exists neither an embracing approach to explain the international distribution of R&D activities nor one to design it efficiently.

The author develops a new model of the R&D subsystem of multinational corporations. Using modern quantitative methods the model determines both the optimal distribution of R&D activities among countries and the optimal assignment of tasks. The empirical test of the model suggests that at present not all multinational corporations show an efficient internationalization of their R&D activities.

The book addresses lecturers and students of international management, innovation management and organization theory as well as scientists and axecutives in R&D management and organizational planing.

Betriebswirtschaftlicher Verlag Dr. Th. Gabler GmbH, Abraham-Lincoln-Str. 46, 65189 Wiesbaden

Management
International Review
© Gabler Verlag 2003

EDITORIAL OBJECTIVES

MANAGEMENT INTERNATIONAL REVIEW presents insights and analyses which reflect basic and topical advances in the key areas of International Management. Its target audience includes scholars and executives in business and administration.

EDITORIAL POLICY

MANAGEMENT INTERNATIONAL REVIEW is a refereed journal which aims at the advancement and dissemination of international applied research in the fields of Management and Business. The scope of the journal comprises International Business, Transnational Corporations, Intercultural Management, Strategic Management, and Business Policy.

MANAGEMENT INTERNATIONAL REVIEW stresses the interaction between theory and practice of management by way of publishing articles, research notes, reports and comments which concentrate on the application of existing and potential research for business and other organizations. Papers are invited and given priority which are based on rigorous methodology, suggest models capable to solve practical problems. Also papers are welcome which advise as to whether and to what extent models can be translated and applied by the practising manager. Work which has passed the practical test of successful application is of special interest to MIR. It is hoped that besides its academic objectives the journal will serve some useful purpose for the practical world, and also help bridging the gap between academic and business management.

PUBLISHING · SUBSCRIPTION · ADVERTISEMENTS

Published quarterly, fixed annual subscription rate for foreign countries: Individual subscription 108 Euro (approx. US $ 112.–), institutional subscription 212 Euro (approx. US $ 219.–), single copy 59 Euro – (approx. US $ 55.–). Fixed annual subscription rate for Germany: Individual subscription 99 Euro –, institutional subscription 206 Euro. Payment on receipt of invoice. Subscriptions are entered on a calendar basis only (Jan.–Dec.). Cancellations must be filed by referring to the subscription number six weeks before closing date (subscription invoice); there will be no confirmation. There may be 1 to 4 supplementary issues per year. Each supplementary issue will be sent to subscribers with a separate invoice allowing 25% deduction on the regular price. Subscribers have the right to return the issue within one month to the distribution company. – Subscription office: VVA, post-box 7777, D-33310 Gütersloh, Germany, Tel. 0049/(0)5241-8019 68/802891, Fax 80 96 20. Distribution: Kristiane Alesch, Tel. 0049/(0) 6 11/78 78-3 59. Reader-Service: Britta Christmann, Tel. 0049/(0) 6 11/78 78-1 29, Fax 78 78-4 23. Advertising office: Thomas Werner, Tel. 0049/(0) 6 11/78 78-1 38. Editorial Department: Ralf Wettlaufer, Tel. 0049/(0) 6 11/78 78-2 34, e-mail: ralf.wettlaufer@bertelsmann.de. Annelie Meisenheimer, Tel. 0049/(0) 6 11/78 78-2 32. Production: Gabriele McLemore, Betriebswirtschaftlicher Verlag Dr. Th. Gabler GmbH, Abraham-Lincoln-Straße 46, D-65189 Wiesbaden, Tel. 0049/(0) 6 11/78 78-0, Fax 78 78-4 00. Internet: Publisher http://www.gabler.de; Editor http://www.uni-hohenheim.de/~mir; Managing Director Dr. Hans-Dieter Haenel; Publishing Director Dr. Heinz Weinheimer; Senior Publishing Editor Claudia Splittgerber; Sales Manager Gabriel Göttlinger; Production Manager Reinhard van den Hövel. Produced by Druckhaus „Thomas Müntzer" GmbH, Bad Langensalza – Contributions published in this journal are protected by copyright.

© Betriebswirtschaftlicher Verlag Dr. Th. Gabler/GWV Fachverlage GmbH, Wiesbaden 2003.

Gabler Verlag is a company in the specialist publishing group BertelsmannSpringer.

No part of this publication may be reproduced, stored in a retrieval system or transmitted in any form or by any means: electronic, magnetic tape, mechanical, photocopying, recording or otherwise, without permission in writing from the publisher. There is no liability for manuscripts and review literature which were submitted without invitation.

ISSN 0938-8249

Have you already visited our **mir** homepage?

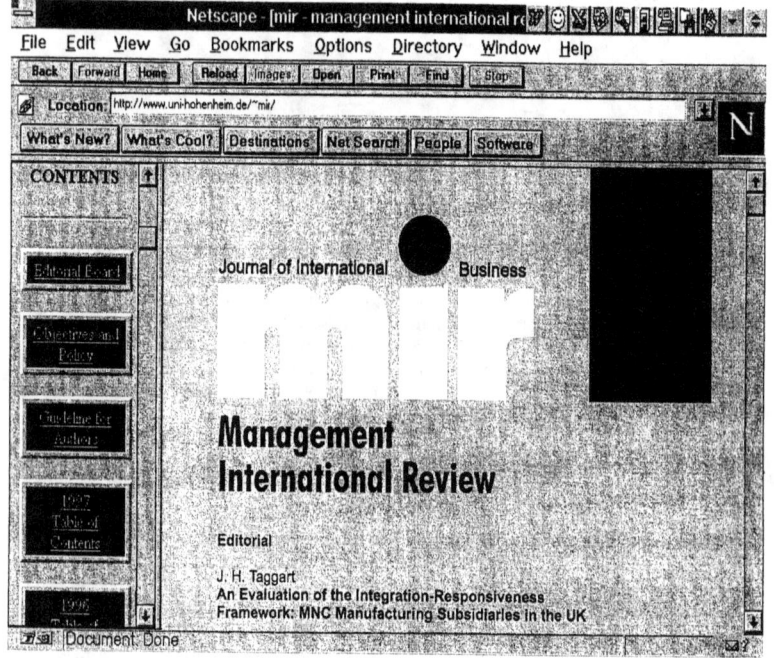

If not, then it is high time you did!

http://www.uni-hohenheim.de/~mir

ISBN 3-409-12447-0
VVA 126/02447

GPSR Compliance

The European Union's (EU) General Product Safety Regulation (GPSR) is a set of rules that requires consumer products to be safe and our obligations to ensure this.

If you have any concerns about our products, you can contact us on

ProductSafety@springernature.com

In case Publisher is established outside the EU, the EU authorized representative is:

Springer Nature Customer Service Center GmbH
Europaplatz 3
69115 Heidelberg, Germany

www.ingramcontent.com/pod-product-compliance
Lightning Source LLC
LaVergne TN
LVHW011958070526
838202LV00054B/4960